# Gone But Not Forgotten

# Gone But Not Forgotten

## Church Leaving and Returning

PHILIP RICHTER and
LESLIE J. FRANCIS

DARTON · LONGMAN + TODD

First published in 1998 by
Darton, Longman and Todd Ltd
1 Spencer Court
140–142 Wandsworth High Street
London SW18 4JJ

ISBN 0–232–52236–7

A catalogue record for this book is available
from the British Library.

Except where otherwise indicated all Scripture excerpts are taken from the
Revised Standard Version of the Bible.

All interviewees' names have been changed to preserve their privacy. Any
resemblance between these pseudonyms and actual individuals is
completely coincidental and unintended.

Designed by Sandie Boccacci
Phototypeset in 9.5/12.5 pt Palatino by Intype London Ltd
Printed and bound in Great Britain by
Redwood Books, Trowbridge

# Contents

# Preface

In the mid nineteenth century the Christian denominations were busy building new churches and developing networks of church schools. The denominations were planning for growth, and this growth included establishing the church colleges to train teachers for church schools. Methodist initiative built Southlands College in London. Anglican initiative built Whitelands College in London and Trinity College in Carmarthen. Roman Catholic initiative built Digby Stuart College in London.

At the end of the twentieth century the church colleges are re-shaping their agenda to serve the changing needs of the churches in a very different religious culture from the one in which they were created. Part of this agenda is to serve the research needs of the churches. As part of the Roehampton Institute, London, Whitelands College, Southlands College and Digby Stuart College have played an important part in the Institute's new Centre for Advanced Theological Research. As an associate college of the University of Wales, Trinity College Carmarthen has created the Centre for Theology and Education. In the present study these two centres have collaborated to address the foremost question confronting the churches at the end of the twentieth century. Why are so many people currently leaving the churches and how might they be encouraged to return?

The Church Leaving Applied Research Project based at Southlands College and Whitelands College within the Roehampton Institute, London, was initially inspired by an approach to the Methodist Church Home Mission Division by a Methodist minister, nearing retirement, who had long been puzzled to know why some regular church goers eventually lapsed. The Home Mission Division subsequently commissioned the Centre for Advanced Theological Research at the Roehampton Institute to undertake research into people's motivation for church leaving. The scope of the enquiry was broadened to include leavers from any church denomination. Philip Richter was permitted by the Methodist

Church to work full-time as director of the project during the academic year 1996–97. The questionnaires were coded and analysed using the SPSS statistical package at Trinity College Carmarthen and University of Wales, Lampeter.

We wish to express our gratitude to the bodies who funded the research, including the Roehampton Institute, the Methodist Church, the Esmée Fairbairn Trust and the Allchurches Trust. We are grateful for the goodwill and help given by Stephen Holt (Rector of the Roehampton Institute) and by the Principals of the Church Colleges, Clive Jones-Davies (Trinity College Carmarthen), Michael Leigh (Southlands), David Peacock (Whitelands) and Bernadette Porter (Digby Stuart).

We have also appreciated the assistance, interest and advice we have received from the following people: Peter Barber, David Gamble, Brian Hoare, Dave Martin, Michael Meech and Stanley Porter (members of the Project Steering Group); Bryan Tolhurst (Methodist Church Conference Office Administrator); John Fulton and Michael Hornsby-Smith (and other members of the University of Surrey, Sociology Department, Religious Research Seminar); Martin Albrow, Kevin Bales and Graham Fennell (Sociology Department, Roehampton Institute, London); David Denney (Royal Holloway College, University of London); Father Michael Hayes (Chaplain, Digby Stuart College); Káren North (research student and principal interviewer); Gerry Foley and Victoria Piggot (interviewers); Angela Pearson (interview transcriber); Judy Adams (telephone calling recruiter); Catherine Calvin, Jeanette Carey, Michaela Ford, Janet Jones, Caroline Lloyd, Alison Runacres and Jane Simmonds (telephone callers); Mandy Robbins (data management); Anne Rees and Diane Drayson (shaping the manuscript); and Jane Lankshear (providing the index).

*Gone but not Forgotten* is offered to *church leaders*, who are looking for practical solutions to church leaving, to *ordinary church members*, who are puzzled why some of their companions drop out, and to *leavers themselves*, who may find their own stories echoed and given a new perspective here.

PHILIP RICHTER
Whitelands College London

LESLIE J. FRANCIS
Trinity College Carmarthen

*July 1997*

# Foreword

There are more than 40,000 churches in England, let alone churches in other parts of Great Britain. Their total budget, taking into account running costs, including salaries of ministers and charitable giving, must be in excess of £500,000,000. Yet the amount spent on research as to how they are doing, what could be improved and what should be avoided can be no more than a fraction of a per cent. Some industrial firms spend 10–15 per cent of their turnover on research: the Christian church barely begins despite the command of its Master to 'Keep watch . . . keep awake' (Mark 13:33–37).

But any research into the life of the church and its impact on people has to be good research. Poor research, by giving an impression of accuracy, can mislead. Anecdote and hunch are no substitute for careful questioning and analysis. Further it has to be done in this country: research from countries like the United States, though thought provoking, can also lead us astray because of the different religious and cultural background.

It is therefore especially timely, towards the end of the Decade of Evangelism, for this book to be written by Philip Richter and Leslie J. Francis. In 1992 I published the result of research into how adults entered the church. Repeatedly I was told, 'You have looked at the front door by which people enter the church; we need information on the back door as well.' This book is the carefully researched answer to that demand. All denominations should be grateful to the Methodist Church for this ecumenical initiative and to the bodies which funded it, for good research does not come cheap.

It is too easy to see both the joining of a church and the leaving of it only in terms of a spiritual journey. This book reminds us again and again that evangelism is a socialising as well as a spiritual process as the inner journey is reflected in the outer journey of changing a lifestyle and joining a congregation. Similarly it shows us that most who leave church do not lose faith. They see their leaving primarily as ceasing to socialise with a certain congregation and ceasing to behave in an expected way.

The results of this research should be pondered long by all church leaders for it has much to teach us. Too often leaders do not have the basic information upon which to base their policies – or they can shy away from the hard work and cost of finding out by saying, 'All we need to do is to pray.' The spiritual must not become a bolt-hole from the reality of life for each must intermingle with and permeate the other.

This research touches every church in the land, for not one can say, 'Nobody has ever left us.' This book is not an easy read, for it challenges too many long-held opinions, and reminds us of too many pastoral failures. We shall find that simple answers are not enough. We cannot just say, 'It is their sin', though it may be for a few. Nor can we say sadly, 'There is nothing I can do about it', because this book shows that many 'leavers' want to return. Church leaders in particular will need courage to look unpalatable facts in the eye. Similarly there will be many ordinary members of congregations who will read this book and understand more fully why their child or friend no longer comes to church with them, and with such understanding should come deeper prayer and a more resolute relationship with those who have left.

This book should come with a health warning: talking all the time about those who have left the churches is right and proper, but depressing. This book rubs our noses in the dirt. But we need also to remember those who are finding new life in Christ and friendship within our churches. This book paints half the picture, the half we prefer not to look at.

JOHN FINNEY
Bishop of Pontefract

# Introduction

## Setting the scene

A satirical cartoon appeared in the *Financial Times* in March 1996. It featured the owner of a burger bar and the minister of an adjoining Methodist chapel both standing at their respective doorways, on a Sunday morning, looking in vain for customers.[1] At this time the emergent BSE crisis had just devastated trade at burger bars, whilst the Methodist Church's latest church membership figures had given rise to fears that the Church might be facing 'meltdown'.[2] Between 1992 and 1995 there had been a 6.8 per cent decrease in Methodist membership; attendance at worship had declined by 9.7 per cent; the number of young people attending on a Sunday had fallen by 19.1 per cent.[3] The prediction was being made that within forty-one years, at the current annual rate of loss (2.47 per cent), the Methodist Church would have zero members.[4]

The Roman Catholic Church had already, earlier that year, reported that Mass attendance was slipping at an even faster rate than Methodist membership. Between 1988 and 1995, numbers attending Mass had dwindled by nearly 200,000; in 1995 alone there had been a 3 per cent drop. Of an estimated 4.5 million Catholics in England and Wales, fewer than one third actually attended Mass in 1995. By the year 2005 attendance at Mass would probably halve. Not surprisingly, commentators were beginning to claim that the Catholic Church was 'losing mass appeal'![5]

By early 1997 it was clear that the Anglican Church was also in danger of steep decline. Official figures revealed that average church attendances in 1995 were 3.3 per cent lower than in 1994; attendance had dropped by 678 people each week, of whom 180 were under the age of sixteen; even Easter communicants had dropped by almost the same number. The number of teenagers presenting themselves for confirmation was now half the level it had been in the early 1980s; between 1994 and 1995 alone there had been a 9 per cent fall. Equally alarmingly, the number of under-sixteen year olds attending Sunday services had dropped by 19,000 between 1992 and 1994.[6] It was tempting to assume that people were simply deserting mainstream churches for more evangelical or charismatic churches. Nevertheless, even amongst charismatic fellowships there was evidence of decline, with 6 per cent fewer adults attending in 1996 than in 1995.[7]

It has been estimated that 1500 people leave British churches each week, not counting those who die, or simply transfer to another church. In 1992–93 78,000 people took up membership in British churches, but an equal number left. Another 76,000 died and left for the Church triumphant (Brierley 1996:8,11).[8] If the results of our own random telephone survey, in October 1996, are representative, they suggest that 62 per cent of the population of England have, at one time or another, attended church 'at least six times a year (not including Christmas and Easter)'. Three out of five of these people, however, no longer attend – some 18.1 million people (based on 1996 projected population figures). Even allowing for the fact that a significant proportion of these may be exaggerating their past involvement[9] or may have attended invol-untarily as a child, there is a considerable number of people in the British population who have either been church members or have been happy to attend a church at some time in their lives, but do so no longer.

Church leaving is a crucial factor in the numerical decline affecting churches. It means that churches are not replacing those who die. Given that in the Church of England, for instance, 22 per cent of church goers are sixty-five years of age or over, whilst there are only 15 per cent in this age group within the general population (Brierley 1991:39), there is likely to be a continuing shortfall, unless churches increase the number of people they recruit and retain those people more effectively.

Church decline is not simply of parochial interest to churches themselves. The drift, whether permanent or temporary, from the churches has clear personal and social implications of crucial importance to the wider welfare of society as a whole. There is growing evidence that church going 'shapes morality'.[10] Religion, it has been shown, influences factors as diverse as substance abuse, social violence, and suicide (Kay and Francis 1996). Conventional religious involvement is positively associated with life satisfaction, personal happiness, physical health and longevity (Levin 1994).

Church going is good both for the health of individuals and the welfare of society. One firm of insurance brokers even offers cheaper car and home insurance to church goers, on the basis that 'the positive lifestyle factors of church members make them a better than average risk'.[11]

Church leaving is by no means a new phenomenon. It has been around in various forms since the very earliest days of the Christian Church. The Parable of the Sower (Mark 4:1–20) recognised that some people drop off because they lose their faith (v. 15); others find being a Christian too costly (v. 17); others are lured away by other interests (v. 19) and, like Demas, are too much 'in love with this present world' (2 Timothy 4:10). It is not a new thing for people to 'fall by the wayside', but, as we shall see, there are some extra reasons for church leaving in contemporary society.

In this book we shall be exploring some of the key reasons why people today drop out of churches. Why do they let their church participation lapse? What causes them to drift away, or to make a sudden break, sometimes after years of involvement? Might they have stayed if their church had understood their needs better? Are some of the factors associated with their leaving beyond their church's control? We consider it is vital to diagnose the problem accurately if churches are to develop effective strategies for responding to this ongoing haemorrhage. This book is not about people's reasons for joining – or not joining – in the first place. That is a separate, although related, question. We have chosen to focus solely on people's motivations for *leaving* churches.

Church decline makes amateur sociologists of us all. Most of the church goers and clergy to whom we speak have their own pet hunches as to why people have dropped out of church going. These range from easily remediable factors to suggestions that church decline derives from the lack of a 'feel-good' factor in British society![12] We should warn the reader that, inevitably, this book is unlikely to substantiate everyone's favourite theories. We conducted a brief survey at the 1996 Methodist Conference to discover what the representatives (lay and clergy) considered to be the principal reasons why people were leaving the Methodist Church. Nearly half of the representatives took part and their replies fell into twenty-five categories, the most frequently cited of which were: objections to worship style, contextual and life changes (such as removal to a new area), social belonging factors, and lack of relevance. We were interested to discover how far the perceptions of these church leaders corresponded to the reasons actually given by people leaving churches. In the event, as one might have expected, there were some evident blind spots. This book invites you, the reader, to put your favourite theories to the test and to take a more objective look at church leaving in all its complexity and variety.

The theories we report here are based on a careful review of the international research on church leaving set against the new sociologically grounded work undertaken between 1995 and 1997 by the Church Leaving Research Project, based at the Roehampton Institute. Further details about the work undertaken by this project are provided in the appendix on methodology. Throughout the following chapters we draw on the qualitative data provided by a series of interviews and on the quantitative data provided by a questionnaire survey. In our qualitative and quantitative studies we have defined church leavers as people who, having attended church at least six times a year (not including Christmas and Easter), had subsequently lapsed to attending church less than six times a year.

## Exploring the causes

In order to make sense of church leaving, *Gone but not Forgotten* has divided the discussion of the causes for leaving into eight broad categories, while acknowledging that people's motivations are generally too complex and various to be simply pigeon-holed into just one category. Each of these eight broad categories has been given a chapter of its own, in chapters three to ten, after the first two chapters have established the wider context for the discussion.

Chapter one begins by setting the question of church leaving within the wider context of commitment in contemporary British society. This chapter asks how much church leaving may be seen as part of a more generalised 'retreat from commitment' in today's society. Is it too simplistic to suggest that nowadays people prefer not to belong to organisations any more, including the church?

Chapter two explores the stages involved when an individual drops out of church going. This chapter takes account of socio-logical perspectives on disaffiliation, often originally based on research into new or unconventional religious movements of various kinds. What are the specific steps that a church leaver takes in the process of disengagement? Is there any single shape to the process of church leaving?

Chapter three examines the theory that loss of faith plays a major part in church leaving. Some commentators suggest that this is *the* key reason for church decline, while others consider that loss of faith is a comparatively minor factor. Have most church leavers stopped going to church as a consequence of losing their faith first?

Chapter four considers the significance of changing social values in the process of church leaving. The first issue to be explored concerns the 'generation gap' between those who have left churches and those who remain. Have church leavers stopped attending because the church seemed to them like 'another planet' or part of a 'past culture'? The second issue to be explored concerns the implications for church leaving of the differences in basic values between different cohorts or generations. Do the so called 'Baby Boomers' and 'Baby Busters' leave church for different reasons in comparison with an earlier generation?

Chapter five considers the relevance of stages of faith development for understanding church leaving. How true is it that individuals grow in faith at different paces? Does the faith development of some individuals outgrow the congregations to which they belonged? Do some individuals leave church because their congregation and minister are too far ahead of their own stage of faith development?

Chapter six examines the effect of changes and chances in the pattern of life on church leaving. How many people leave church almost unintentionally as a consequence of some other changes in their life, like moving house, changing job, getting married, experiencing marital disruption, needing to care for ageing parents, or responding to the needs of growing teenage children?

Chapter seven explores the responsibility of parents and of upbringing for church leaving. How many church leavers had been forced to attend as a child and just could not wait to break out of the habit? How many church leavers had been introduced to church as children but had lacked the good solid example of parental commitment to their church and had themselves simply followed suit?

Chapter eight examines the theory that some people leave church because they find the cost of commitment too high. Do churches drive people away by making increasing demands on their time, or by making increasing demands on their money?

Chapter nine considers the view that people leave churches because those churches fail to live up to their expectations. When expectations are not fulfilled, disillusionment sets in resulting in church leaving. How many church leavers blame their church for letting them down in some way? How many people leave out of frustration with the worship they experience, with the pastoral care they receive, with the teaching to which they are exposed, or with the style of leadership they witness?

Chapter ten considers the role of broken relationships and conflict in precipitating church leaving. When churches fail to offer their members a sense of belonging to a closely knit and supportive community, do they prefer to get up and leave? Do more people choose to leave the church because they perceive the threshold between the church and the outside world to be too high? Or do more people choose to leave the church because they fear that the church is failing to draw a sufficiently clear line between Christian values and the values of the outside world?

Chapter eleven returns to the questionnaire data provided by our survey of church leavers to address two specific questions. First, is it possible to identify the main precipitating reasons behind church leaving and to distinguish these main precipitating reasons from the host of other associated factors? Second, is it possible to detect a relationship between the causes cited for leaving church and an individual church leaver's likelihood of returning? Answers to both of these questions may have significant implications for pastoral strategy.

Finally, after attempting to diagnose some of the factors underlying church leaving, chapter twelve explores some possible remedies. How might churches enhance their strategies for encouraging leavers to return? How might potential leavers be retained? The book ends with some practical pointers.

# 1    A Retreat from Commitment?

How far is church leaving part of a more generalised 'retreat from commitment' in today's society? In this chapter we shall be setting our somewhat parochial reflections on church leaving within a wider discussion of the concept and practice of commitment in contemporary British society.

The 1996 Church of England report on young people and the Church, *Youth A Part* (General Synod Board of Education 1996), took some consolation from the fact that although there had been substantial decline in church attendance and church-based youth work 'similar patterns of declining attendance can also be found in secular organisations' (p. 13). For instance, the number of Scouts and Guides (fourteen- to seventeen-year-olds) meeting in churches had decreased by 15.8 per cent between 1987 and 1993. The report also took comfort in the 'sensitivity and commitment many young people have to issues of justice, peace and the environment' (p. 165). This is, however, only part of the picture. The commitment of young people to these kinds of issues does not necessarily translate into political engagement. As one of the report's eighteen-year-old interviewees put it: 'I want a society which is fair and [where] there is equality, peace and harmony – I would like to go into politics but I don't know if I am right or left' (p. 10).

## Commitment today

Both Labour and Conservative parties are finding it difficult to recruit young blood. Membership of the Young Conservatives has dwindled to 7,500 or less from, at one time, over half a million members.[1] Only 5 per cent of Conservative party members are younger than thirty-five. Their average age is over sixty-one and almost half are over sixty-six. The picture is only slightly better for Labour. Research published in the early 1990s concluded that the average age of Labour Party members was forty-eight and that there were over three times as many members aged over sixty-six as under twenty-five. Since Tony Blair became leader, the Labour Party has begun to grow and its average age appears to be dropping, but both parties have shrunk considerably in the last decades. The Conservative Party now has only one member for every six it had in the 1950s and, in the same period, membership of the Labour Party has dropped by nearly two thirds, although the Labour Party currently claims to have an 85 per cent retention rate,[2] with twice as many members joining as leaving. Fluctuations in membership of the Labour Party are partly attributable to the transition that has occurred from a ward-level to a national-level membership system; this has, on the one hand, identified much 'dead wood' and, on the other hand, offered a much less cumbersome way to join.

There is evidence, however, that where young people have joined the Conservative Party or Labour Party they show appreciably greater commitment to the party than older members. Under-twenty-five-year-olds in both parties are more committed to their political principles than to winning a general election. They are also more likely to place themselves further to the right or left, respectively, on their party political spectrum (Seyd, Whiteley and Parry 1996:6).

It would be too simplistic to suggest that young people are mostly apathetic and unwilling to commit themselves. If they are fired by the right issue young people do become active, but not necessarily within traditional political parties. Young people tend to be more interested in single-issue campaigns, focused on issues such as the environment or animal rights, where they can see immediate effects. For instance, up to a third of eighteen- to thirty-four-year-olds claim to have been involved in protests to do with animal rights (Wilkinson and Mulgan 1995:103). It is true that young people may be alienated from mainstream politics and traditional institutions, such as the Church, but they do have considerable confidence in voluntary organisations, which are generally perceived as 'committed and trustworthy and at ordinary people's level' (Gaskin, Vlaeminke and Fenton 1996:3). At least 40 per cent of young Britons claim to be involved in voluntary work of one sort or another. Sometimes this is a one-off event such as Comic Relief; sometimes this is regular involvement in, for instance, visiting an old people's home. The estimated value of their work in financial terms is £3.4 billion per year (Gaskin, Vlaeminke and Fenton 1996:5). Unlike their older counterparts, young people are likely to be larger-hearted and less judgemental about who deserves help. Research reported in 1997 by The Trust for the Study of Adolescence demonstrated that young people were 'certainly more involved in campaigning and voluntary activity than the popular image . . . would suggest'.[3]

If commitment to those in need is still alive and well amongst the young, how does the notion of commitment fare amongst society generally? Commentators on the British economy have detected a fundamental lack of commitment within the British financial system. Shareholders are increasingly uncommitted to the companies they own. Will Hutton, in his best-seller *The State We're In*, has provided a damning indictment of the financial system's obsession with liquidity and short-term profitability. He concludes that this 'makes it difficult to sustain the committed relationships which are at the core of productivity growth' (Hutton 1996:158). In 1995 the Royal Society of Arts held an inquiry into the foundations of long-term business success. It concluded that a company must have a commitment to sustain five key relationships: with shareholders, workers, customers, suppliers and the community.[4] At present the British financial system encourages companies to concentrate almost exclusively on their relationship with investors. The pervasive threat of takeover deters long-term investment and companies are milked for short-term profits. Will Hutton detects a permanent tension in our economy 'between the desirability of forming committed relationships where both parties co-operate and don't cheat on each other – and the temptation to cut and run, attempting to find a better deal elsewhere' (Hutton 1996:252). Worker commitment is hard to elicit when pay and job security takes second place to the need to generate rapid and high dividends for shareholders.

One of the most visible areas of British society in which there has been an apparent retreat from commitment is that of personal relationships. Since 1971 the marriage rate has dropped by more than half. Every two marriages in 1994 were matched by at least one divorce. Those who cohabit have no greater success in sustaining their relationships. Cohabiting couples are four times as likely as married couples to split up. Where a cohabiting couple later get married they still have a higher risk of divorce than those who have not lived together prior to marriage (Wilkinson and Mulgan 1995:72). Increasing numbers of women are choosing never to have children of their own: as many as 22 per cent of women presently aged between twenty-seven and thirty-two.[5] To what extent has the notion of commitment to partner or children changed or gone out of fashion? Could personal relationships be the last bastions of commitment in a society where employers and employees seldom perceive their relationship in such terms? Does this help to make for unrealistically high expectations of the commitment required in personal relationships?

A sea change is occurring in people's attitudes to marriage. The nature of the marriage commitment has changed radically. As recently as the 1950s marriage was regarded as a key British *institution*, in which the married couple fulfilled their respective roles as homemaker and breadwinner and were expected to stay together through thick and thin. Nowadays marriage is increasingly seen in terms of a *relationship* that promises 'emotional intimacy, mutual affection and sexual fulfilment' (Wilkinson and Mulgan 1995:69). Marriage is entered upon and kept going as long as it delivers these goods and the couple will settle for nothing less. Couples commonly refer to each other as 'partners' in 'a relationship'. By this they mean that they have close, ongoing emotional ties to each other, that they are each committed to maintaining the quality of the relationship and that each has the expectation that, as a result, they will become more authentic and fulfilled human beings. A successful relationship will involve enduring effort by each partner to win the trust of the other and to communicate effectively.

The nature of this relationship means that any commitment the partners give to each other is bound to be conditional. The desire for a life that offers self-actualisation and fulfilment tends to take centre stage and to have priority over marriage vows. 'Hollow shell' marriages, where partners stay together merely for the sake of their children, are becoming far less common. As Anthony Giddens, one of the foremost sociological commentators on this phenomenon, puts it: '[such a relationship] is only sustained in so far as it generates sufficient psychic returns for each individual . . . the possibility of dissolution . . . forms part of the very horizon of commitment' (Giddens 1991:187). Paradoxically, couples can still have long-term expectations, at least at the point when they get married, because, although they are aware that marriages are prone to fail, they trust that 'it's not going to happen to me'.

The new attitudes to personal relationships that we have been describing do not automatically signify a retreat from commitment.

Changes have occurred in the notion of commitment and these have not necessarily been unwelcome. On the one hand, there is the prospect that marriage will become a less patriarchal institution and will more adequately reflect the intention of the Marriage Service that husband and wife should 'give themselves to each other in love'.[6] On the other hand, given that so much more is expected of marriage, it should come as no surprise if marriages fail at a high rate and churches, amongst others, are needed to help pick up the pieces.

It is tempting to want to try to correlate decline in church involvement with a more generalised retreat from commitment in British society. As we have seen, the general picture is mixed and by no means suggests that commitment is everywhere on the wane. In any case, there may be more perennial problems facing voluntary organisations and, specifically, churches in their eliciting of commitment and it is to these that we now turn.

By their very nature most voluntary organisations face difficulties in evoking and sustaining their members' commitment. Ruth Finnegan's book, *The Hidden Musicians: music-making in an English town* (Finnegan 1989), is an elegant account of musical groups in the Milton Keynes area. She relates how the Sherwood choir was always concerned about its fluctuating membership. There was always membership loss as schoolchildren grew up and went away to college, as people moved to a new area, as work and family commitments changed, as illness or advancing years made it difficult for people to get out in the evening, as transport arrangements broke down, as people forsook the choir for another that sang their kind of music. The actual attendance at rehearsals was often much less than the paid-up membership. 'Week after week the conductor had to look at empty chairs . . . and every now and then was provoked into launching into that well-known diatribe in all musical groups: castigating those who were there with the irresponsible absence of those who weren't' (Finnegan 1989:239). It is worth noting that diatribes of this sort are also well-known to church goers! Ruth Finnegan concludes that 'the wonder was not that people left but that so many continued to turn out to rehearsals and concerts season after season' (Finnegan 1989:239).

Ruth Finnegan also describes the difficulties involved in keeping bands going. Bands, especially small ones, depend on substantial commitment of time and energy, often at antisocial hours. Any number of things could get in the way of that commitment, such as someone moving away, marriage, parenthood, job pressures, or internal disagreements. Players would often complain that the others simply 'weren't pulling their weight'. She could have been describing many a church. No voluntary group, churches included, can afford to take their membership's loyalty for granted. As Ruth Finnegan's account demonstrates, continued participation can never be guaranteed, not least because people have to handle a host of other commitments.

Most voluntary organisations, including churches, have always faced particular problems in sustaining commitment: this is by no means a new phenomenon. Arthur Black, for instance, attributed church decline in the Putney and Roehampton area of south-west London in the late 1920s to such diverse factors as the First World War, the gramophone, cinema, wireless, improved social and travel conditions and 'intellectual unsettlement' (Black 1928).

Churches fit into the general category of 'voluntary organisations' and, as we have seen, there are similarities between churches and other voluntary organisations in terms of the difficulties both face in retaining members. Churches, however, differ significantly in other respects, not least because of their basis in a transcendental belief system. Leaving a rock band, for instance, is unlikely to raise questions about the meaning of life! Commitment to a church is, in theory, if not always in practice, a much more serious business.

## Defining church membership

Churches vary in terms of the degree and nature of formal commitment expected from those who belong. As we shall see, there is no common blueprint, even amongst the mainstream Churches. There is a sense in which everyone in England is a member of the Church of England, unless they choose to opt out. Everyone lives within an Anglican parish and has a legal right to be married in their parish church. Until as recently as the mid 1950s around three out of every five infants born in England were baptised at Anglican fonts, but this did not necessarily translate into adult commitment. One frequently cited definition of practising Anglicans is derived from a rubric in the 1662 *Book of Common Prayer* which specifies that 'every parishioner shall communicate at the least three times in the year, of which Easter to be one'. As a consequence of this rubric the Church of England has for a long time monitored the

number of Easter communicants. Traditionally confirmation has
been regarded as the gateway to communion in the Church of
England. In theory, therefore, the confirmation list should provide a
key to the wider concept of membership. There are three problems,
however, with this theory. The names of those who have been
confirmed are not kept on any kind of membership roll. In an
ecumenical generation communion is now offered to communicant
members of other denominations. Following the Knaresborough
report in 1985[7] in some places children have been admitted to
communion before confirmation.

Another definition of Anglicans is based on membership of the
Electoral Roll. Once an Anglican reaches the age of sixteen he or
she is eligible to be placed on the church's Electoral Roll. This
entitles him or her to vote at the annual general meeting of the local
church, which elects members of the Parochial Church Council, as
well as representatives to Deanery Synods. Those joining the Electoral Roll are expected to be regular church attenders, although
there is no minimum level of attendance stipulated. In practice
most people on Electoral Rolls attend at least monthly, if not
weekly.

According to these various definitions people may cease to be
Anglicans by one of three main routes. First, they may choose to
change their church allegiance by joining another denomination.
Secondly, they may choose to lapse from the practice of receiving
communion at least three times a year. Thirdly, they may allow
their names to lapse from the Electoral Roll. The Electoral Roll
is revised every six years and if, at that time, individuals are
not attending regularly they may miss the opportunity to fill
in the necessary form to continue on the Roll. Theologically, the
Church of England prides itself on being a broad Church, encompassing everything from Anglo-Catholicism to Charismatic-
Evangelicalism. It is relatively easy to drift out of a Church such
as the Church of England when it does not have a strong sense of
just who is and who is not a member.

Free or Nonconformist Churches have a much more developed
membership system. Indeed the concept of 'church membership'
is very much a Free Church concept. It was the Methodist Church
that first attempted to count its members accurately (Bruce
1996:28). Its methodical approach to keeping track of its members
has persisted. Methodists become members of the Church through
Baptism and Confirmation. Confirmation is also known as being

'received into full membership'. Their names are then held on the membership roll of their local Methodist church. Should they move away their membership is meant to be transferred to their new church. Every three years detailed statistics of Church membership are presented to the Church's governing body, the Methodist Conference. Methodists receive membership tickets at least once a year, which include a printed reminder of their obligations. Within the Church, members commit themselves to 'worship, holy communion, fellowship and service, prayer and Bible study, and responsible giving'. In the wider world there is a commitment to work out their faith in daily life, to offer 'personal service in the community, the Christian use of their resources, and the support of the Church in its total world mission'. If Methodist members fail to meet these obligations their membership may be rescinded and they may be classified as 'ceased to meet'.

Methodists are expected to take part in what is known as the Covenant Service, a special annual opportunity to 'renew their Covenant with God'. This service, usually held early in January, contains a profound reaffirmation of commitment, not unlike the vows a person would make at ordination or upon reception into a religious community:

> I am no longer my own, but yours. Put me to what you will, rank me with whom you will; put me to doing, put me to suffering; let me be employed for you or laid aside for you, exalted for you or brought low for you; let me be full, let me be empty; let me have all things, let me have nothing; I freely and wholeheartedly yield all things to your pleasure and disposal.[8]

To a Roman Catholic the concept of 'church membership' is puzzling. Once one becomes a Catholic one remains a Catholic, unless one commits a sin grave enough to warrant excommunication. Entry to the Church takes place through baptism, either as an infant or as an adult. Adult baptism is now often preceded by what is termed the Rite of Christian Initiation of Adults (RCIA). Infant baptism is followed by First Communion (at about seven years old) and Confirmation (at about fourteen years old).[9] Catholics are expected to attend Mass at least every Sunday and on major feast days, unless they are prevented by illness or travel. There is however no register kept of those who are or are not carrying out this obligation. Those who do not attend Mass regularly would usually term themselves 'lapsed Catholics', although the tendency nowadays is for the Church to describe them as 'resting', in the hope that this state will not be permanent. To be a Roman Catholic is to take an active part in the worshipping community.

By contrast, Protestants tend to see their faith in more individualistic terms. Believing in the 'priesthood of all believers', Protestants have tended to regard church going as less important than the relationship between the human being and his or her Maker. Protestant theology, albeit unintentionally, has tended to breed the assumption that 'you can be a perfectly good Christian without going to church'.

As well as denominational differences, there are also variations according to the theological style of a given church or local congregation. Conservative, more sect-like, churches tend to have much stricter membership expectations than liberal churches. Although almost all churches expect some degree of doctrinal orthodoxy from their members, amongst conservative churches a very high premium is set on toeing the party line; there will be a strong boundary between church and secular world; and sacrificial giving, for instance, in the form of tithing of disposable income, will be the norm. Where people fail to meet these expectations their continued membership is in doubt. Paradoxically, conservative churches do not necessarily get all that concerned about the phenomenon of church leaving. There are two main reasons for this. First, they prefer to channel their energies into evangelising the unchurched; worrying about the back door can divert attention from the front door. Secondly, if the less committed choose to leave then, by definition, this means that those who remain are the more committed; it is better to lose people on the periphery of the church, if this leaves a more committed core.

Alongside the commitment of individuals to their church and God there is mutual commitment by churches to their members. This commitment reflects the covenant promises of God: 'I will be their God, and they shall be my people' (Jeremiah 31:33). Some churches appear to regard the bonds they have with their members as indissoluble, 'till death us do part'. Others seem to see the church's commitment as provisional and revocable if their members fall away. One is reminded of the short-termism characterising British industry. Could it be that the second type of church is behaving too much like a fickle management that 'pulls the plug' when their investment fails to show immediate returns? At least one of the covenants in Scripture had no strings attached (Genesis 9:16) and was meant to be everlasting; some churches seem to be better than others at reflecting this!

The absence of common criteria for church membership presents problems for researchers attempting to analyse church leaving. What level of commitment is sufficient to classify someone as belonging to a church in the first place? What cut-off point should be selected, below which a person is deemed to have left the church? Within a denomination such as the Methodist Church it is relatively easy to identify church leavers as those who have ceased to be on the membership roll. Other Churches, as we have seen, do not operate such hard and fast membership categories. In practice, researchers have tended to settle on measures of church *attendance*, rather than membership. The Gallup Organisation define the 'unchurched' American as someone who has 'not attended services in the previous six months other than for special religious holidays, weddings, funerals or the like'. In our own study we have adopted Dean R. Hoge's (Hoge, Johnson and Luidens 1993) more rigorous definition of the church dropout as someone who has reduced his or her church attendance to less than six times a year (not including Christmas, Easter, weddings or funerals).

Whatever rule of thumb is chosen, it is by no means certain that the dropout will understand him or herself in such terms. People often still claim to belong to a church, even when they hardly ever attend. Indeed C. Kirk Hadaway (1990) has coined the term 'mental members' for these church dropouts. Equally, those who attend a church regularly may not be as fully committed as they seem. Sociologist Rosabeth Kanter (1972) has pointed out that commitment takes place at three levels. First, there is commitment to the organisation, which involves investment of at least some of the person's time, energy and money. Secondly, there is commitment in the form of close emotional ties to a person's fellow church members: 'Blest be the tie that binds our hearts in Christian love.' Finally, there is commitment to the official beliefs and values of the church, as interpreted by the leadership. If a person is committed at one level this will tend to lead on to commitment at another, but it is possible to be committed at only one level. Several of the church leavers interviewed in the Roehampton Survey recognised that their previous level of commitment to the church had never been particularly extensive.

For Justin Wyatt, a student and son of a vicar, 'It was just one of those things, I had to get up on a Sunday and go ... it had no meaning for me ... it was just habitual and now that's past and I can move on to something else.' Peter Kendall, a middle-aged ex-Methodist television producer, went to Sunday school (Junior church) and chapel from the age of five. He became a local preacher at seventeen years old, but left church the following year. 'I think I came into the church out of habit ... and that [it] was a social thing, because it wasn't really a spiritual thing ... looking back, I don't think I was really a spiritually committed Christian. I believed in God as a sort of thing that you did, and I would pray, and I would go to church, and I would occasionally get emotional about it, but I don't think it registered that deeply with me.'

Donald Harper, who was once a Roman Catholic priest, described himself as agnostic and, when pressed, was unsure whether he ever believed in God: 'I think one of the telltale signs is that I very rarely prayed, in the sense of with a deep conviction that I was communicating with a personal God.' David, a Methodist Youth Club member, who was about to be confirmed, confessed that, 'I don't know [if there's a God], I don't know what my belief is at all.'

Charles Mason, a solicitor who grew up in Wales, had got involved with the church choir as a boy, 'because being a good Welsh boy I had quite a good voice ... but I think my interest was not religious, it was social really and it was just one of the things that one did on a Sunday'. When his voice broke he left the church. Later on, influenced by his fiancée, he became a regular church goer and now sits on the Parochial Church Council. He reported that the church is a 'huge cultural and social part of our lives ... because the children go to church school, [because of] the families we meet who are involved with the school, the families we meet in the congregation: a big chunk of our social life revolves around the church'. He is honest enough to admit, however, that 'it's probably right to say that I don't think of my church attendance in terms of faith very much if at all'.

## Listening to the statistics

Our questionnaire respondents were asked to look at a battery of 198 statements and to identify those which best described why there had been a dropping off in their church going. The questionnaire asked a set of five questions specifically designed to survey aspects of *commitment*. In table 1.1 we separate the respondents into two categories, depending on whether they left before the age of twenty or later in life. The figures in each column are percentages of that category.[10]

**Table 1.1:   Retreat from commitment**

|                                                                         | Under 20 % | 20 and over % |
|-------------------------------------------------------------------------|:----------:|:-------------:|
| I never felt very committed to the church                               | 53         | 30            |
| It was easy to drift in and out – my church did not expect strong commitment | 35    | 30            |
| My main motivations for going to church were not religious              | 41         | 20            |
| It was unclear what commitment to the church involved                   | 21         | 15            |
| I believed that you do not need to go to church to be a Christian        | 68         | 75            |

The statistics show that factors concerned with commitment were more likely to be cited by those people who had left before the age of twenty. Over half the people in this category reported that they had *never* felt very committed to the church, while two-fifths of them recognised that their main motivations for going to church during the early years of life were not religious. Nearly one-third of all respondents agreed that it was easy to drift out of the church. Well over two-thirds believed that church going was unnecessary for Christians.

Another item in our questionnaire was designed to check the extent of church leavers' current participation in non-church groups or organisations. The question asked was this, 'In how many non-church groups or organisations have you participated during the past year (e.g., sports, educational, community)?' The

replies are set out in table 1.2. The statistics presented in this table
show that over two-thirds of leavers had participated in a non-
church group or organisation during the previous year. This suggests that for many individuals church leaving is not part of a
generalised retreat from involvement in voluntary organisations.

Table 1.2:   Current participation in non-church groups or
organisations

| N groups | % participating |
|---|---|
| None | 32 |
| One or two | 38 |
| Between three and five | 23 |
| Between six and ten | 5 |
| More than ten | 2 |

## Summary

It has become a truism to suggest that declining commitment
within churches is simply a reflection of a wider retreat from
commitment in British society. As we have seen in this chapter, the
evidence is mixed. Young people are willing to commit themselves,
but not necessarily to traditional institutions such as churches.
People are still willing to commit themselves in personal relationships, but their commitment to each other is more tentative.
Voluntary organisations, such as churches, by their very nature
have always faced particular problems in sustaining commitment.
Churches vary as to the degree and nature of formal commitment expected from those who belong. In some cases commitment
may not have declined: it may not have been there in the first
place.

# 2    The Leaving Process

There is no single shape to the process of church leaving. In this
chapter we shall be exploring some of the directions the leaving
process may take. We shall be taking account of sociological perspectives on disaffiliation, often originally based on research into
new or unconventional religious movements of various kinds, and
we shall be selecting those elements that shed most light on the
processes involved for church leavers.

Two main approaches have been taken by sociologists of religion
studying disaffiliation. The first, built on analysis of role playing,
relates particularly to those leavers who would not recognise themselves as having been converted or deconverted. The second is
based on models of conversion and deconversion, breaking down
the leaving process into specific stages with particular causes.
Leaving may or may not involve loss of faith. Disaffiliation does
not necessarily mean deconversion – either because individuals
may not claim to have been converted in the first place or because
they are still committed to their faith, if no longer to their church.

## Role playing

Sociological *role theory* presupposes that human behaviour is
shaped to a large extent by the expectations of others. People, as
it were, look over their shoulder to try to gauge what is or is not
acceptable behaviour in a given context. A person's sense of self
is developed and reinforced by looking in the 'mirror' of other
people's reactions. In their everyday lives people play a series of
roles, such as spouse, child, employee, motorist, and even as church
goer. Part and parcel of the role of church goer is such activities
as regular attendance at services, willingness to sit through
sermons of varying length and quality, readiness to sing hymns
without too much self-consciousness, commitment to support the
work of the church through regular gifts in the collection plate,

avoidance of blaspheming or dirty humour, at least whilst in the company of other church goers, and generally behaving not all that differently from fellow church attenders. Roles are sometimes merely acted out without much personal engagement. On the other hand, roles may be accepted and thoroughly internalised by the individual, serving to mould his or her personality.

People sometimes go to church not out of faith commitment or religious experience but on an experimental basis, to see if there is anything in it. They may assume the role of church goer and be virtually indistinguishable from other more committed church goers, but eventually shed the role in the absence of anything that convinces them to play the role for real. Others may not at first realise anything is amiss: people's discontents and doubts can easily be camouflaged by their continued playing of the role. On the whole churches do not continually question people's motives and it is rare that other church goers will be waiting to 'catch them out'. Gradually, these leavers begin to recognise that they are merely playing a role and, for the sake of their own personal authenticity, become 'ex church goers'.

'I was just going through the motions', 'I was pretending to be someone I wasn't', 'I was living a double life', our interviewees confessed. Alison Matthews, a social worker and Catholic leaver in her twenties, told how she had decided that, 'I couldn't carry on going to church in this regular way . . . for months I'd been going to church just out of habit . . . I would have to stop going to Mass.' Postgraduate student, Arron Coates, another young Catholic leaver, said, 'I used to make a thing of going and sitting down the front and [participating] very loudly, and then, whenever there's a [liturgical] response, I'm there bellowing, and I thought, "God, why?", because I don't enjoy that, I just want to go and pray in my own little way.' For Gareth Wilkinson, an ex-Methodist computer software executive, now in his mid-forties, the church going role was dropped when he began to lose faith in his erstwhile role models in the church: 'I began to be aware of some real hypocrisy; some of the characters in the church who were in [the] position to me of really strong, correct people – role models, examples, you know – actually in my experience turned out not to be that.'

Even where an individual is not simply acting a part, but fully identifies with the role of church goer, there is always the possibility of being caught in role conflict, which may be resolved to the detriment of the role of church goer. A person's role as caring parent may put constraints on how time is used on Sundays. In a society in which there is perceived danger for children in being out alone it is not uncommon for parents to spend considerable time chauffeuring their children around to their friends or leisure activities. A person's role as employee may interfere with the role as church goer. With substantial deregulation of Sunday trading employees can find themselves under increasing pressure to work on Sundays. For students this may be an economic necessity.

For some people, the weekend is the only spare time they have, after working late into the evening during the week to hold down increasingly precarious jobs. Gareth Wilkinson explained that time on Sundays was highly contested, because, 'I will often go Sunday evening to Friday evening and not see my children . . . I'll be sleeping in the same house as them, but I will often get back from work after they have gone to sleep, and leave before, always leave before, they get up.' He goes to the United States on business twice a month, typically travelling at weekends. 'The company I work for is Jewish . . . so of course they defend Saturday, not Sunday. I often spend Sundays on aeroplanes to New York, and, for the same reason, I often spend Friday night on the way back.' When he is at home on a Sunday his role as caring parent is paramount. 'My children are all active in their own interests and unfortunately a lot of those interests are only available on a Sunday, like the boys playing cricket – that is Sunday morning.' The role of church goer has to compete with the role of parent, or shopper, or sports player, or visitor of elderly parents and so on. For the divorced church goer Sunday may be the only day for access to children.

## Stages of deconversion

It is a useful rule of thumb to say that the way in to church going generally affects the way out of church going. Analyses of conversion and deconversion suggest that, where a leaver has become a church attender as a result of conversion, their leaving will very likely be marked by a process of deconversion. Conversion is probably best defined as a radical transformation in the way an individual interprets reality, entailing a fresh view of the world, a new set of relationships and altered personal identity. As one convert famously put it in the well-known hymn, 'Amazing Grace', 'I once was lost, but now am found'.

Deconversion constitutes either a journey out of faith or conversion to another more plausible religious way of interpreting reality and self-identity. In the process, much of what happened at conversion begins to go into reverse, although it would be too simplistic to describe it as merely a mirror image. Sociologists of religion have identified various stages or levels of withdrawal from religious groups. Although these are not necessarily directly transferable from one study to another, we will highlight certain key elements relevant to church leaving. Our own analysis is informed by an influential study by Skonovd,[1] who has broken down deconversion into the following sequence: (1) crises of belief; (2) review and reflection; (3) disaffection; (4) withdrawal; (5) transition; and (6) relocation. We will now explore and expand on each of these stages in detail, with illustrations from our own interviews with church leavers.

### Crises of belief

These are precipitating factors, first setting the process in motion. Disillusionment may be provoked by a variety of possible factors. People may be over-exposed to secular culture, calling into question Christian perspectives on the world. They may become frustrated that the church is not having any immediate impact for good in the world. People may become impatient with a conflict-ridden or uncaring church, that fails to be the loving community they seek. They may become aware of inconsistency between what leaders preach and what they do. Such disillusionment is quite different from the passing doubts most church goers experience on a regular basis.

Our interviewees were often keen to separate out the key precipitating factors in their church leaving. They would often make it clear that this or that was an important factor, but not the real trigger. Richard Elliott, an Anglican senior citizen who had lost faith in his church, but not in God, and who had switched to another church, told us: 'I didn't leave because I didn't believe, or because I had a row with somebody ... it was because I felt the teaching was all wrong, not at this particular church, but nationally.' Justine Sullivan, a teacher and an ex-Anglican in her twenties, related how studying for a theology degree had caused her to question her faith, but she insisted her principal reason for leaving was exposure to a New Religious Movement: 'If I was to look back and say why I left, it would be partly because of college, questioning things, but ... mainly it was because of this awful experience I'd had in this [cult].' One of a group of Methodist young people described his friend's church leaving: 'Well, like I say, he plays badminton, that's usually on Sundays, but I think it's probably deeper than that.'

### Review and reflection

At this stage people begin to weigh up the pros and cons of continued involvement. This is often a gradual process of carefully and judiciously considering their options. In this respect it closely resembles the process of conversion. John Finney, in his survey of those who had recently made a public profession of faith, *Finding Faith Today*, found that on average 69 per cent of people described their journey into faith as gradual, whilst only 31 per cent regarded it as sudden or datable (Finney 1992:24). Even where a sudden decision to leave is taken, it is likely to have been preceded by previous heart-searching.

In Richard Elliott's case it took twelve years for his misgivings about Anglican morality to 'come to the boil'. Deborah Clarke, a middle-aged former Anglican lay reader, said her leaving 'was a gradual process of getting angry, and not understanding why I was angry'. Justin Wyatt described how he got 'more and more fed up with [church going] over time ... in the last few years I started to feel uncomfortable, but after a certain age I stopped taking part: I wouldn't join in any prayers or anything like that'. Justin went on to relate what he termed the 'sudden step' of finally choosing not to attend at all. Our interviewees often described a moment when 'the penny dropped'. Matthew Williams, a freelance graphic designer and formerly a member of a New Church, told how he realised 'that the whole thing was a joke ... I suddenly saw through it all ... I couldn't carry on in the church with this history, which ... had made me so unhappy for so long'. Alison Matthews had been troubled by aspects of the Catholic Church for some time but had not thought of leaving: 'It was very strange the way it happened ... as I sat through Mass ... it hit me so suddenly ... just like a flash ... in a moment I knew I had to stop going.'

Church leaving is typically gradual and involves a period during which a person's religious identity, lifestyle and understanding of the world is re-evaluated. After weighing up the alternatives he or she chooses to leave. In some cases he or she will feel the pull of other belief systems. In the case of Peter Kendall, an ex-Methodist, it was when he became secretary of the local branch of the Young Socialists that he gained an ideological reference point outside the church: 'the church really had given me my only ideology, up until that point, and at fifteen I began therefore to compare and contrast . . . and question what I had taken for granted for so long.' Similarly, Alison Matthews, after getting to know people of other faiths for the first time in her life, approached her Catholicism in 'a more questioning way . . . I started to look at [church] people's attitudes towards . . . non-Christian religions, and I didn't like what I saw there'.

Justin Wyatt told how he would 'test the water': 'I wouldn't go one week and see how it was, and see what reaction I got from Mum and Dad.' After testing out the alternatives he concluded: 'I didn't get any benefits from going to church, or I didn't feel any benefits, whereas if I got to spend time with people, or go for a walk, I found it much more productive.' Some leavers initially explore alternatives within the Christian Church but ultimately discover they have run out of viable alternatives. Russell Briggs, an ex-leader of a House Church, who had in the past belonged to the Anglican Church and a United Reformed church, described how there was 'nowhere to go' when he became disillusioned: 'I had sort of gradually gone out onto the periphery . . . I didn't want to go back, there's no way . . . I've stopped calling myself a Christian.' In his account of the fall of the Sheffield Nine O'Clock Service Roland Howard suggests that one of the reasons why people were sometimes reluctant to leave in spite of its many failings was the absence of places to go 'for *disillusioned*, dis-illusioned charismatics' (Howard 1996:151).

It is more difficult to leave if people belong to a church that has exercised considerable control over the way they lead their lives. If the whole of life is almost completely bound up with church there may be few viable alternatives to which to turn. If people are dependent on the church for their friends, as well as their meaning in life, it takes considerable courage to leave. The process involves self doubt and apprehension as to whether this is the right move to make and leavers are commonly left with ambivalent feelings towards their former church. There are mixed emotions and attitudes towards their church, which has at one time, if not any longer, been a source of comfort and meaning. This is not unlike the ambivalence shown by ex-partners after marital separation and divorce: the ending of formal commitment does not do away with the more satisfying features of the relationship, nor does it render the previous involvement purely negative. Steve Wright's analysis of three New Religious Movements comes to similar conclusions: leavers had salvaged something positive from their involvement and 'one sensed ... a felt [sense of] loss of closeness, unity, and co-operation in achieving shared goals or ideals' (Wright 1987:88).

In weighing up the pros and cons of leaving, a good deal of ambivalence is shown towards the church. In some cases negative verdicts on the church are very nearly outweighed by recognition of the positive benefits received from church going. Very many of our interviewees retained highly positive memories of their churches. Even Sharon Chapman, an ex-Methodist in her early thirties, who deeply resented church going being forced on her by her parents, had a great fondness for the church she had left. 'I believe in the Methodist way of going to church, because it's very relaxed and I enjoy it, and I've still got friends from there ... It was a really lively church ... and it was good fun ... I've no bad memories of the church at all.' Arron Coates spoke of the 'pride' he still has in the church: 'It's a faith I was proud of, and [I] still have tinges of pride, because there are people doing a lot of good.' Rosabel Abass, a young ex-Methodist nurse with West Indian roots, credited the church for having given her a stable framework for her life: 'I was taught the Ten Commandments ... how to talk to people, how to treat people ... If I hadn't gone to church I'd probably be out there on the street, begging money.'

Suzanne O'Leary, a young Catholic student interviewed in Northern Ireland, movingly credited the church with providing opportunities for education for Catholic girls like herself: 'The Catholics were the underdogs in Northern Ireland for a long time ... if it wasn't for the good old Catholic Church we wouldn't be educated.' On a rather more mundane level, Russell Briggs, now a computer salesman, credited his church with having taught him useful transferable skills which now help him in his business decision-making: 'I have to make hundreds of decisions every day about people ... I do it because I just go by what I feel within: that's the way that I live, and I'm very grateful for that way, and I wouldn't have got there if I hadn't been in the church.' Donald

Harper, ex-Catholic priest, summed up leavers' ambivalence towards the church when he said: 'It's got good sides and great gifts, but, my, sometimes it's answerable for an awful lot ... on the other hand, it is answerable for all sorts of good things too.'

In some cases the influence of non- or ex-church goers or non-believers is an important factor at this stage. The catalyst for Justine Sullivan leaving her New Religious Movement was a conversation with an ex-member: 'I just felt something that I had within me that I felt was the truth, and I felt really happy about it, left me ... and I went out of that house feeling a totally different person.' For ex-fundamentalist Edward T. Babinski his fundamentalism had gradually intellectually unravelled once he had exposed himself to non-fundamentalist literature and to correspondence with former fundamentalists: 'I began to consciously admit that perceptions and questions raised by *non*believing thinkers agreed with some of my own' (Babinski 1995:221).

## *Disaffection*

Here the emotional ties between individuals and their church begin to weaken. Studies of conversion have frequently highlighted the importance of friendship and emotional bonding in cementing people's loyalty to the church. Indeed this often predates conversion at the level of belief and conviction. The *de*conversion process equally involves gradual distancing from emotional involvement with the church. Bit by bit, bonds are broken with those within the church and new ones are formed outside. At this stage often the decision is taken to leave and planning begins as to how this will be carried out.

For Peter Kendall the process of disengaging from his church friends took some time: '[For three or four weeks after leaving] I turned up after the service was over to meet friends, as they came out.' In fact quite a few of his friends left at the same time, which reduced the need to sever emotional bonds. Matthew Williams, who had left a New Church, spoke of the difficulties disengagement brought for his children: 'My daughter would like to go to church and one of her best friends is from the church ... [the family] used to be good friends of ours and they've gone totally nutty about the Toronto Blessing ... I can't handle them actually, and they can't handle me either, because I question everything all the time ... We've gone very different directions really.'

## Withdrawal

This is the point at which departure takes place – the 'parting of the waves' as one of our interviewees put it. Sometimes there is a final trigger, often the accumulation of previous factors: the 'final straw for the camel's back'. As one of the clergy we interviewed put it: 'Something happens which makes them realise that they've actually had enough of it . . . It could be something that appears in the press, or the ordination of women, or the fact the vicar wants to turn the pews around, or introduces new hymns . . . [and] people just think, "I can't, I've had enough of this." ' Arron Coates compared the 'little problems' he had with the church to a dripping tap: 'If things constantly tap on you, like torture . . . where they strap you up and drop a raindrop on your head, sooner or later you'll crack.' In some cases an event becomes the 'final excuse' to leave. Paul West, a middle-aged ex-Anglican civil servant, told how, 'the fact that my mother became ill . . . probably gave me the excuse . . . the break'.

Some leavers drift away; especially if they have had a history of gliding in and out of a number of organisations. Some drifters want their leaving to be quiet and unnoticed and prefer not to have to answer others' well-meaning questions. Other leavers will be more overt about their leaving, in some cases making what is known as a *declarative* departure, in which they state publicly their reasons for going, which are often tied up with reasons of anger or frustration. This is not unlike marriage partners who suddenly announce to their spouse that the marriage is over and they are leaving. Where someone leaves, with a public flourish, because of a point of principle, this is likely to be a seasoned church goer who has finally given up trying to win the church over. There were particular reasons why Peter Kendall, one of our interviewees, felt the need to make his leaving very public. In his late teens, Peter recognised his lack of faith, but by then he was already a Methodist local preacher. He had to find a way to distance himself publicly from that role. He chose to challenge a group of Methodist university students on mission in his church to a public debate – and sided with the opposition! 'I needed them there to be able to make that sudden announcement, in that sort of way, that I no longer believed.'

A declarative departure may also help to release some of the inevitable tension accompanying separation from the church: leaving may be experienced as liberating, but also as a source of anxiety and uncertainty. For Alison Matthews it felt like leaving home, 'and that brings with it a lot of excitement, but a certain amount of trepidation and a bit of fear as well, stepping out into the unknown, stepping out from where you feel comfortable, where you know and are known'. Deborah Clarke felt a mixture of guilt and joy as she started to do different things on Sundays: 'walking in the park and feeling guilty that I wasn't at church, [but] I was aware of the amount of earthy energy and joy and all those sorts of things which were lacking in my church feelings'.

### Transition

After leaving, individuals enter a period of transition, during which they shed their previous identity and attempt to find new sources of meaning and purpose in their lives. Not surprisingly, it is not uncommon for people to feel considerably disorientated and as if they are in limbo, cut adrift from the safe and familiar. This is not unlike the experience, described by anthropologists, of people undergoing rites of passage such as initiation rituals, weddings or funerals, who go through a disturbing, although ultimately creative, *liminal* threshold to the new phase of their life. Hannah Ward and Jennifer Wild have explored some of the parallels in their book *Guard the Chaos: finding meaning in change*. Leaving a church involves 'losing a home, a place that gives us a framework, or container, where we can be who we are and express who we are' (Ward and Wild 1995:36) and in this case there is no rite of passage, no church service to help manage this time of transition.

Ex-House Church leader, Russell Briggs, felt profoundly disorientated after leaving. 'My life [used to be] so filled with purpose, in fact it was greatly difficult, after living this life which was going to transform the Church, if not the world, to end up selling computers ... It wasn't quite in the same ball park, and it was very difficult to adjust to that initially.' Nicholas White, a freelance producer, who had left a Baptist church, reported that initially 'we were a bit bruised and battered and didn't quite know where to go from there'. Donald Harper, an ex-Catholic priest, acknowledged that his experience of finding himself in limbo was ultimately creative: 'having lived my life very much with a plan and a framework and that in a way disappearing – so, no money, no job, nowhere to live – that was quite an interesting experience, probably the most valuable experience of my entire life really.'

## Relocation

The final phase of deconversion is reached when, and if, people successfully complete the previous stage and begin to make sense of their lives without reference to their former church and when they start to build up new social relationships. This leaving behind of religion does, incidentally, add to the difficulties faced by those seeking to study church leavers: this may be a phase of life that people have effectively bracketed out of their mind.

At this stage the leaver starts to substitute new friends and activities. As a group of young Methodists remarked sadly: 'They've just gone off with different people now.' Until new ties are established the leaver may feel as though he or she does not fit anywhere. Richard Elliott, after leaving his parish church on a point of principle, found himself questioning his own actions: 'If you're in a minority you have to ask yourself, because there are few of us that think like this, [is there] something queer about us . . . we must be wrong, because more people think this way than we think.' Where leavers have belonged to a church that has, to a large degree, insulated them from the 'outside world', it is doubly difficult to establish new relationships. As Russell Briggs put it: 'You lose touch with the real world . . . you get locked into your own system and leaving it was weird . . . because you're suddenly going back into the big wide world and I didn't realise how cut off I'd become.'

It is important not to interpret the stages of deconversion we have identified in a deterministic fashion, as if once started on the process there is no going back. People are not passive victims of social forces. It is true that conversion has sometimes been understood in overwhelmingly passive terms. St Paul's dramatic conversion on the Damascus Road, which leaves him lying on the ground temporarily blinded and brings about a sudden change of heart and lifestyle, has become the benchmark of conversion in the western world. St Paul's experience is likely, however, to have been somewhat different from that of many modern converts who play a much more active part in their conversion process, experimenting, exploring and first trying on their new identity for size. As for conversion, so for deconversion which does not simply suddenly happen to the individual, but is the result of measured choice on his or her part.

The process of church leaving is by no means necessarily a one-way street. One stage does not lead inexorably on to the next. In his survey based on the United Methodist Church in the United States, John Savage concluded that once a person decides to drop out of church he or she will then wait for six to eight weeks before re-engaging their time on other activities. This period of *limbo*, as Savage terms it, serves two main functions. First, it enables people to begin to adjust to their loss of church involvement and, secondly, it tests out whether anyone from the church will come and follow up their lapsing from church going. If someone from the church does take the trouble to contact them within this six to eight week period and 'meets their needs and listens to their aches and pains' (Savage 1976:98) the process may be reversible.

Sometimes our interviewees remained angry that the church had not followed up their departure. Samuel Hartley, a Catholic who left church for a time because of his homosexual orientation, felt that the church had a responsibility 'to really get hold of people and say, "look, why are you not going to church, what's happening?" Nobody did it to me and I felt, at times, quite angry about that.' Charles Mason, who left a charismatic Anglican church, was disappointed that there was no follow up at all, except 'one chap in our [house] group who did get in touch with me and it turned out that he wanted to sell me life insurance!' Where leavers occasionally set foot inside their former church they are sometimes puzzled at people's responses. When Alison Matthews paid a visit to church some people asked 'where have you been?'; when she told them of her spiritual search that had taken her beyond Christianity some voiced their disapproval, others 'wished her all the best'. 'Nobody really said, "Oh, I think you ought to come back." In fact, for a moment, I felt almost as though no one really cared that I'd left,' Alison told us. She appreciated the response of one priest who said, 'I don't want to know where you've been, I'm not going to ask, but it's lovely to see you', which 'showed a great respect for [her] personal freedom to be a member of the church or not'.

### Listening to the statistics

Respondents to the questionnaire were asked 'Would you describe your dropping off from church attendance as gradual or sudden?' In table 2 we separate the respondents into two categories, depending on whether they left before the age of twenty or later

in life. The figures in each column give a percentage breakdown
of that category.

Table 2:  The leaving process

|                     | Under 20 % | 20 and over % |
|---------------------|:----------:|:-------------:|
| Gradual             | 33         | 48            |
| Can't say either way| 9          | 10            |
| Sudden              | 58         | 42            |

The statistics show a somewhat different pattern for the leaving
process among the two categories of respondents. The leaving
process is more likely to have been sudden among those who left
under the age of twenty than is the case among those who left after
their twentieth birthday. Conversely the leaving process is more
likely to have been gradual among those who left as adults in
comparison with those who left under the age of twenty.

## Summary

In this chapter we have been exploring aspects of the leaving
process from two different sociological perspectives: focusing, first,
on the roles people play and then, secondly, on how people con-
struct their view of reality. We concluded that there is no one
typical leaving process: the process will vary according to the
type of leaver. The process tends to be gradual, measured and
cumulative; it is often accompanied by a desire to avoid personal
hypocrisy; it may be reversible (especially within six weeks of
leaving); it may be followed by a period of 'limbo'; but generally
it results in ambivalent (often surprisingly positive) attitudes to
the church. People's 'way in' to church going tends to be predictive
of their 'way out'. Sociological approaches highlight some of the
processes at work. However, one must not lose sight of the individual and his or her own motivations for leaving. In the next
chapter we shall begin looking at some of the specific reasons
people themselves give for leaving.

# 3   No Longer Believing,
   No Longer Belonging

In this chapter we shall be considering to what extent loss of faith plays a part in church leaving. Some commentators have claimed that loss of faith is the primary reason for church decline. Steve Bruce concludes that 'those who explain their lack of church involvement by considerations other than a lack of belief are fooling themselves or fooling the researchers' (Bruce 1995a:47). Evidence for this view is, however, difficult to come by. Certainly, studies of church leavers do not generally rate this factor particularly highly. Michael Fanstone, in *The Sheep That Got Away*, was surprised to discover that only 7 per cent of respondents to his survey had left church because of 'God issues' and because 'they felt in some way that God had let them down' (Fanstone 1993:79–80). In none of Annabel Miller's interviews with church leavers for *The Tablet* did she find a dissatisfaction with the vision and demands of Jesus.[1] Dean Hoge's studies of North American Catholic dropouts concluded that most were 'as religious as ever' and that 'for the majority, the act of dropping out of Mass attendance was not a matter of turning their backs on religion' (Hoge 1981:90). J. Russell Hale, in his study of North American 'unchurched', categorises some as 'true unbelievers' but claims that this category in his survey proved to be the smallest (Hale 1977:84).

It is not surprising that loss of faith does not appear to play much part in church leaving in the United States. Opinion polls suggest that 94 per cent of Americans believe in God, compared with 69 per cent of Britons (Greeley 1992:55). Those leaving churches in the United States because they are atheists or agnostics may prefer to avoid the stigma involved in owning up to the fact. By contrast, lack or loss of faith is far more common in Britain and may, conceivably, be a more important factor in church leaving on this side of the Atlantic. The 1991 *British Social Attitudes Survey* reported that just over 60 per cent of Britons had 'always' believed

in God, compared with approximately 90 per cent of those in the
United States. In Britain 16 per cent had once believed but did so
no longer. Significantly, when believers were asked how close they
felt to God, almost a quarter reported that they felt 'not close at
all'. Of those who described themselves as 'religious' very few
described themselves as 'very' or 'extremely' religious.

Religious belief does not, of course, automatically translate into
church going. The *British Social Attitudes Survey* reported that only
16 per cent of Britons 'attend a service two or three times a month',
compared with 43 per cent of Americans. These figures suggest,
on the one hand, that loss of faith is more likely to figure as a
reason for church leaving in Britain and that owning up to loss of
faith will be less embarrassing; and, on the other hand, that at least
some of those who belong to churches may have little faith to lose.

## Believing without belonging?

It has become fashionable to describe religion in Britain as a matter
of 'believing without belonging'. The phrase has been popularised
in a book by Grace Davie (1994), although its pedigree goes back
to at least Carl Dudley (1979:3), writing in the late 1970s.[2] The
majority of Britons tell opinion pollsters that they believe and
that they have religious experiences, but relatively few belong to
Christian churches. At first sight this might suggest that, although
people have disengaged from churches, they may continue to
'believe without belonging'. If one looks in a little more detail,
however, at the content of those beliefs, it rapidly becomes clear
that they are not necessarily close to the beliefs of mainstream
Christianity. A 1968 study cited a conversation that highlights some
of the differences:

> 'Do you believe in God?'
> 'Yes.'
> 'Do you believe in a God who can change the course of events
> on earth?'
> 'No, just the ordinary one.'[3]

A 1987 survey found that more people believed in a rather vague
higher power – 'some sort of spirit or vital force which controls
life' – than in a personal divinity.[4] According to a Gallup Poll in
1982 only 43 per cent of respondents agreed that 'Jesus Christ is
the Son of God'.[5] The religious belief of those who are not church

goers may be more akin to superstition than to orthodox Christian belief. It is true, however, that those who have once been church goers may well retain more orthodox beliefs, unless, of course, their exposure to the church was short-lived or only as a child. Given that so many people in Britain, whilst not participating in churches, lay claim to religious belief it is unlikely that complete loss of faith underlies much church leaving. On the other hand, one key measure of Christian faith is a person's willingness to engage in religious activities. Steve Bruce draws on the analogy of a person who claims to be a 'football fan': 'if he is not a member of a supporters' club, cannot tell you which team he supports, has not been to a match for twenty years, never watches football on television, cannot name any well-known players and never plays football himself then "football fan" is here being used in an unusual manner' (Bruce 1995a:47).

## Atheism

Ultimately one can only take the leaver's word as to why he or she has left. Where church leaving is associated with loss or lack of faith, it is important to distinguish between different kinds of unbelief. Atheism, first, needs to be distinguished from agnosticism. The agnostic is simply unsure whether religious truth claims are true; the atheist rejects them. It is easy, however, to overlook the fact that there are different kinds of atheism, such as: (1) philosophical atheism; (2) experiential atheism; and (3) transitional atheism. We shall look at each of these in turn:

### Philosophical atheism

Atheism of this sort is usually the result of a conscious decision to reject the truth claims of religious faith. Instead of reflecting indifference, this is often the focus of strong feelings and convictions. The philosophical atheist has seriously engaged with the God-question and has concluded either that God does not exist or that this is not a God worth having. One of our interviewees, Samuel Hartley, told how at Catholic boarding school he 'saw [Christianity] as being a good way of life, but certainly many of the other teachings ... didn't make any sense'. Perhaps the best known example in literature is that of Ivan in Dostoyevsky's *The Brothers Karamazov*, who considers that if eternal harmony is bought by the innocent suffering of children 'we cannot afford to pay so much for admission, and therefore I hasten to return my ticket of admission' (Dostoyevsky 1958:287).

Michael Fanstone's survey of church leavers interviewed a man who had been a prisoner of war: he had 'seen a lot of suffering and did not see how there could be a God' (Fanstone 1993:79). Sometimes God is replaced by something else that offers a sense of meaning and purpose to that person's life. For the biologist Richard Dawkins (1986), who rejects religion, it is science which replaces God; for others God may be replaced by a political ideology or a social ideal. It is often assumed that the growth of scientific ideas has tended to promote atheism. Since the great nineteenth-century clash between Charles Darwin and Bishop Samuel Wilberforce, religious beliefs have always tended to lose the contest with scientific theory. In fact, the influence of science has probably been somewhat more subtle than this. Nowadays, thanks to science, people take for granted that the world can be controlled in a predictable manner by technology; in a world of exponentially powerful computer technology and advanced genetic engineering, there may appear to be little room left for the activity of God. Faith in science – scientism – has tended to take the place of faith in God.

Belief is easier to sustain if one is part of a community of like-minded people. If the rest of the world believed that the earth was flat it would be extremely difficult to continue believing that the world was spherical. However true people's beliefs, if they find themselves thinking differently from the majority in society, there is every temptation to conform to the majority viewpoint, on the basis that so many people can't be wrong. Belonging to a church helps to confirm and reinforce people's faith, as they mix with those of like mind. No one in contemporary society, however, can spend all their time with like-minded believers. As soon as the television is switched on or the newspaper opened another world beckons in which God has been marginalised. Children with religious beliefs may find it difficult to sustain them in the face of a largely secular school curriculum.

One of the young people whom we interviewed confessed that he kept his church going secret, 'because in RE lessons there's always people saying it's all a load of rubbish [and] the Bible's all fiction'. An individual's belief is affected by his or her reference groups or 'plausibility structures', as sociologists term them. People who have left church, for reasons other than loss of faith, often find that their faith tends to become more vulnerable once it is separated from participation in a believing community. Samuel Hartley told us: 'a sense of the divine does grow stronger within the church ... and the sense [of God] got weaker, being away from the church ... and God became very very small.'

Rejection of Christian belief, or at least traditional concepts of God, has motivated some radical feminists to leave the church in recent decades. Christian beliefs have been discarded by them as irredeemably patriarchal and oppressive of women. The theologian Daphne Hampson (1990), for instance, believes that her feminism is incompatible with Christianity and now describes herself as a 'post-Christian'. The feminist philosopher Beverley Clack (1994:7) asks:

> Can the Christian God be described in non-sexist language? Can alternative female images for God be found in Scripture? Can the Christian concept of God expand to contain female images for the divine? If it cannot, it would seem that the only appropriate action women can take is to leave the church.

Deborah Clarke, an ex-Anglican lay reader, told us that one of the factors in her leaving was her 'getting in touch with a much more feminine sort of spirituality' which was at best 'tolerated' by the male incumbent with whom she became 'angrier and angrier'. Other feminists prefer to stay and to try to change the church from within or at least to keep their options open. Feminist theologian Alison Webster suggests that women who feel marginalised by Christianity should make strategic choices to define themselves as either Christian or ex-Christian, depending on their circumstances (Webster 1995). It would be a mistake, however, to assume that women are leaving churches *en masse* on feminist grounds. Rebecca Jones' in-depth interviews with ten women who have left Christianity uncovered just one person who had left because she was a feminist and because she could not reconcile this with Christian faith (Jones 1995:3).

### Experiential atheism

In a study of young people in Germany Karl Nipkow (1988) identified the following types of objections to Christian faith by church leavers. The first objection is that God had let them down and could not be relied upon to guarantee the goodness of the world: 'When I prayed to him, because I was in a jam, he never helped me'; 'I do not believe in God, for I had to witness so many terrible things, accidents in which good friends of mine died, catastrophes, etc.' The second objection is that religious explanations of reality did not seem to be plausible. Religious explanations of the origin of the world were rejected, as were beliefs in life after death. The third objection is that God is a 'nice fantasy' but does not really exist. Although God-symbolism may be comforting and inspiring, 'these are [just] stories they tell'.

As Karl Nipkow's study shows, some atheism is more accurately described as *experiential* rather than philosophical in nature. Atheism may result from intellectual questioning or it may be rooted in people's experience of life and in their loss of a sense of the goodness and love of God. As the book of Job demonstrates, disappointments, misfortune and tragedy can threaten the faith of even the strongest believer. Martyn Evans, an Anglican vicar, told us of one of his parishioners, a fervent Evangelical, 'who believed that God was very much in charge, and when his daughter became very seriously ill it created such radical questions about his faith and his understanding of God that, being a man of some integrity, he just didn't feel able to keep on going to church'. 'Where is God? This world is really screwed up', Barry Johnson recalls asking himself when he dropped out of church going as a teenager at the time of the Vietnam War (Roof 1993:12). Paradoxically, those same experiences can either distance people from God or bring them closer to God. John Finney (1992:50), in his survey *Finding Faith Today*, noted that bereavement and suffering were amongst the factors people reported as important in becoming a Christian. Equally, sadly, such experiences can lead to loss of faith.

## Transitional atheism

This form of atheism occurs during a person's growth in faith and is a natural and usually temporary part of his or her faith journey. As we shall explore later (chapter five), it is possible to understand a person's religious development in terms of a sequence of different stages. When the passage is being made from one stage of the journey to the next certain concepts of God may be rejected. The child may throw out God along with Father Christmas and fairy godmothers, only to arrive one day at a more developed concept of God. The adolescent will go through a time of doubt and searching, indeed it has been suggested that there should be a special adolescent rite of passage to allow and affirm the 'vision quest',[6] most appropriately on St Thomas' Day!

One of our interviewees, Donald Harper, an ex-Catholic priest, explained to us that he had decided to leave the priesthood in his mid-forties, shortly after his mother had died. After leaving, he received counselling and felt that his counsellor had got to the heart of the matter when she had suggested 'when your mother died, your God died' or rather 'when your mother died your idea of God died'. 'The more I think about that,' he said, 'it's actually true and I think what I'm agnostic about is the God of the Christian tradition, namely a personal, creating, loving God.' Although he had thoroughly enjoyed being a priest he had never developed a personally owned idea of God, independent of that inherited from his mother, and his busy vocation had masked 'a sort of an emptiness on the inside'. He had recently come to recognise that his 'God' had been too intellectual and that 'God is not a problem to be solved, He is a mystery to be enjoyed'. Naturally, it is not always easy to separate transitional atheism from other more permanent forms. Any form of atheism may turn out to be transitional: only time will tell.

Some, but not many, of the church leavers whom we interviewed reckoned that loss of faith had been the crucial factor in their church leaving. Paul West, once heavily involved in the running of his parish church and local Deanery, suddenly realised, 'I don't really believe in this. I don't believe in what the Church is saying.' He had once believed and he acknowledged that everyone had occasional doubts, but he recognised that, 'if I really believed in it I'd still be going, whatever the niggles'. Other church leavers explained that they had never had any faith in the first place to lose. Justin Wyatt, a vicar's son, was emphatic that he had simply played a role: 'I didn't go because of any feelings I had . . . I don't believe in God.'

Just as religious conversion can sometimes take an experimental form, whilst potential believers 'dip their toe in the water', atheism can also be something that is 'tried out for size' only to be found ultimately unsatisfying. 'I tried out claiming atheism', one leaver told us (Deborah Clarke). Another noted how when people 'come against problems they will actually turn [back] to religion . . . it takes a lot of problems and stuff to realise that you have the belief, you just weren't practising it earlier' (Madeleine, Northern Ireland).

Sometimes church leavers feel that they must distance themselves from God, as well as the church, because they feel that their values and lifestyle are incompatible in some way with a continued relationship with God. Samuel Hartley, a Catholic leaver, did not know how to deal with his nascent feelings of homosexuality and felt unable to acknowledge these in his prayer. 'Previously,' he said, 'I'd sort of given everything to God . . . but then when the homosexual thing came up I sort of distanced myself from Him, because I, possibly without realising it, had a sense that He didn't like it.' Although leavers may feel bound to try to distance themselves from God, they do not necessarily then feel alienated from God. As Samuel Hartley put it: 'I thank God that throughout all my life there has not been one moment when I felt, "He's totally left me." ' In his lowest moments he had contemplated suicide but, 'the thing that kept me back from those sort of things was a real sense of God, and thinking, "If I kill myself He's going to be there watching wherever I am next." '

## Keeping faith

Taking leave of the church does not necessarily have to mean taking leave of God. Even where church leavers have had traumatic experience of life's tragedies and injustices, their faith in God is not automatically eradicated. It emerged that the underlying reason why Arron Coates, a young ex-Catholic, had left church was because he felt intensely angry at God. Two years previously Arron had been best man at his cousin's wedding.

> He's had a really hard life and he's never got what he's deserved and it's always really bugged me, because I'm much more gifted. He's not had a happy upbringing, a very difficult home life. He's not very bright. He's had difficulty with jobs and with relationships and it seems like anything that can go wrong with someone has gone wrong. None of his brothers would be his best man because they didn't like his wife, so I had to. He's never got what he's deserved . . . He's very kind-hearted, very sincere, he keeps up his faith, and looks after my gran and family.

Arron's sense of injustice increased when his cousin's wife gave birth to stillborn twins.

> I really found it very difficult to deal with, because, first, there was [the question] of what people deserve in life and I really felt they deserved more, and, secondly, because he's, against all the odds, maintained his faith, and probably shouldn't have . . . because he's really had nothing back for it . . . It seems like they're continually getting slapped down and kicked down, and then they have to try and get up, and then they get slapped down again. And then you see other people around them that are just dealing in greed and hate and not practising any sort of moral values at all . . . The funeral of two unborn kids was really disturbing . . . and I think it really knocked the wind out of me faith-wise . . . and that's what brought about my current spell of inactivity in the church.

He seemed to be expressing his anger at God by taking it out on the church. 'You've got to take it out on something,' he said. God's existence was not called into doubt, merely God's ability to act justly and with a sense of 'fair play'. In spite of everything Arron still considered himself to be 'a person of faith'.

Church leaving may be followed by a period of intense self-questioning, during which faith may be re-examined and alternative world-views tested out, only to result in leavers eventually reappropriating their faith. Alison Matthews, a Catholic leaver, told us that she had initially been very attracted to the Baha'i faith and had questioned whether Jesus was anything more than 'just a prophet'. It was at Christmas that, 'The realisation came to me that Christ is more than just a prophet . . . I know I am a Christian, and that I love Jesus, and I believe in the divinity of Jesus . . . That's where I am now.' She does not, however, any longer expect any one faith to have all the answers.

Our interviewees were often at pains to reassure us that their church leaving was not to be equated with loss of faith. 'I see God and church as quite distinct', Arron Coates told us. Russell Briggs emphasised that his relationship with God was not affected by leaving: 'I'd had an experience of God, which changed my life, and he's never left me and I've never left him. I left the church. It's a different thing altogether. I wouldn't put the two things at all together.' Sharon Chapman, an ex-Methodist in her early-thirties, had left church to assert her own identity in the face of

parents who had pressurised her to attend church. She was keen
to make clear that she had not lost her faith: 'I do believe, and I'd
like to go, but I've still got that bit of rebellion in me.'

The faith that is claimed by leavers is not necessarily merely
intellectual assent that God happens to exist. In the case of Gareth
Wilkinson, an ex-Methodist, he was not only 'sustained by belief
in God' but also influenced by 'the values and aims and objectives
that are articulated by the Christian faith, which ... are a very
good basis on which to try and live your life ... and to try and
interact with others'. In spite of a heavily pressurised business
schedule, he found time for involvement in projects working with
disaffected young people in the socially troubled area in which his
office was based. Continuing faith in God is sometimes associated
with sporadic visits to church, but not at service times. Suzanne
O'Leary told us how every so often she would 'nip into the
church ... just to say "hello" and see if He's still there ... just to
craic [chat]'. Dorothy King told how she loved to visit churches as
a tourist with her atheist husband: 'I was always a bit in awe of it
in a way ... I just always would walk up the centre [aisle] and
feel I belonged.'

The distinction drawn by many church leavers between leaving
the church and leaving belief in God, is reflected in a further
separation that church leavers often make, between religion and
spirituality. Whilst they are usually happy to describe themselves
as *spiritual*, they are less happy to term themselves *religious*. They
are not alone in this. David Hay has discovered that most university students when asked to write down the words they associate
with *religion* and *spirituality* overwhelmingly connect religion with
the institutional church and with such things as conventionality,
boredom, bigotry and being old-fashioned. Spirituality, on the
other hand, has much warmer associations: 'love, inspiration,
wholeness, depth, mystery and with personal devotions like prayer
and meditation'.[7]

To be spiritual is to be 'more personal and empowering and has
to do with the deepest motivations of life' (Roof 1993:77). The
spiritual person is someone who has a heightened sense of being
part of, or in contact with, the rest of reality. As Russell Briggs,
one of our interviewees, put it: 'Many people are finding a spirituality quite outside the church – it's got nothing to do with
hierarchies and all that kind of thing, it's spiritual.' Alison
Matthews spoke of being on a 'spiritual search' and of 'still

working towards something' after having left church. Spiritual questing can take place within or without the church. This preference for describing oneself as spiritual, rather than religious, suggests that church leaving may be associated with profound changes in contemporary culture which have changed the way people express their beliefs. We move on, therefore, in the next chapter to explore the motivations of those church leavers who have not lost their faith, merely changed it or concluded that it was incompatible with traditional church going.

## Listening to the statistics

Our questionnaire respondents were asked to look at a battery of 198 statements and to identify those which best described why there had been a dropping off in their church going. The questionnaire asked a set of thirteen questions specifically designed to survey aspects of *loss of faith*. From this set we have chosen eight typical questions, reflecting the general spread of responses. In table 3 we separate the respondents into two categories, depending on whether they left before the age of twenty or later in life. The figures in each column are percentages of that category.

The statistics show that factors concerned with loss of faith were

**Table 3:   No longer believing**

|  | Under 20 % | 20 and over % |
|---|---|---|
| I lost my faith | 45 | 29 |
| I doubted or questioned my faith | 58 | 42 |
| A questioning faith did not seem acceptable to the church | 38 | 30 |
| I became aware of alternative ways of thinking or living | 72 | 45 |
| I felt God had let me down | 10 | 9 |
| So many people fight each other in the name of religion | 66 | 64 |
| Many of the church's teachings were illogical or nonsensical | 59 | 34 |
| The church's teachings were difficult to reconcile with modern science | 61 | 37 |

more likely to be cited by those people who had left before the age of twenty. At a stage in life when people tend to become more aware of alternative ways of thinking or living, Christian belief was most likely to be questioned on intellectual and philosophical grounds. Those who left before the age of twenty were more likely than those who left as adults to have concluded that the church's teachings were illogical, nonsensical or difficult to equate with modern science. Nearly two-thirds of all respondents were scandalised that so many people fight each other in the name of religion. About one-third of all respondents had felt that a questioning faith did not seem acceptable to the church.

## Summary

In this chapter we have explored some of the ways in which loss or severe reduction of faith can motivate church leaving. We have noted that leavers may never have had a faith commitment in the first place. Alternatively they may have lost their faith or may find that it presently fails to connect with the rest of their life and has become meaningless. Sometimes this is a reaction to personal tragedy or trauma or a sense that God has let them down in some way. Many church leavers disengage on other grounds, however, and claim still to believe in and experience God (without belonging). Their spiritual quest persists.

# 4    Changing Values

It is quite common for church leavers to report that church seems like 'another planet' or appears to belong to a 'past culture', that social change seems to have passed the church by. There is often a significant 'generation gap' between those who have left churches and those who remain. In this chapter we shall be examining some of the far-reaching shifts that have occurred in cultural values during the last four decades. We shall argue, first, that these changes have had an important part to play in making a whole generation less likely to attend church and, secondly, that this generation brings different expectations to church going and to church leaving. Strictly speaking, we shall be talking about two generations: the so-called 'Baby Boomers' and 'Baby Busters', the latter otherwise known as Generation X. As we shall see, Boomers and Busters share many characteristics, but differ in other important respects.

## Baby Boomer values

In the 1960s and 1970s commentators began to recognise that teenagers were not only leaving the church for time-old reasons, such as adolescent rebellion, but also because of sea changes in cultural values (Roof, Carroll and Roozen 1995:245). If we define Baby Boomers as anyone born between 1945 (Roof, Carroll and Roozen 1995:ix) and 1960 (Ritchie 1995:16), then Baby Boomers were exposed during their most formative years to immense cultural upheavals, such as new musical forms, extensive illicit drug taking, the permissive society, the greater availability of higher education, intense political idealism and unrest, and the growth of New Religious Movements. Even those who did not become 'flower people' or go to Woodstock or demonstrate in Grosvenor Square were affected by the 'counter-cultural' values of the Baby Boom generation. American youngsters dropped out of church in proportionately greater numbers than before (Roof 1993:56); those most affected by the value-shifts are least likely to have returned to church (Roof 1993:171). Baby Boomers have a distinct generational outlook on life, moulded by the events of their late adolescence and early adulthood. We shall now map some of the most significant of the Baby Boomers' new values.

Boomers have a distrust of leaders and institutions. American Boomers' experience of the Vietnam War convinced them that military and political leaders cannot be relied upon. Justified civil rights demands met with state violence. Even university administrations were slow to admit change. Boomers treated many of society's institutions with great scepticism. The family was perceived as a bourgeois relic. The Church, with its hierarchy, rules and regulations, was a means of class oppression. In later decades Boomers have mellowed somewhat, not least because they have needed to support themselves, often holding down well-paid jobs within the very companies they once ridiculed. Their suspicion of institutions remains, however, and leaders have to earn their trust – and that includes Church leaders.

Peter Kendall, an ex-Methodist Boomer, told us how his suspicion of institutions, including the Church, had been stimulated by Ivan Illich's writings: 'Institutions often get [their] purposes diverted, because they create other agendas, because the people in them are in competition for power and whatever . . . and all sorts of things that get in the way . . . Institutions demand loyalty of you . . . Ideas become less important [than] the survival of the institution . . . That had an impact on me . . . I had doubts about the institutional delivery of an idea.' Alison Matthews, a young[1] ex-Catholic, echoed Peter Kendall's rejection of the Church as an institution: 'I look at the main focal power base of the Catholic Church, which is the Vatican, and there's gold and there's wealth and there's wonderful works of art there and that angers me . . . Religion is used to create power for certain individuals.'

Donald Harper, an ex-Catholic Boomer, told us how the process of leaving began when, as a theological lecturer, he started to feel increasingly uneasy about the 'divine' nature of the Church and its doctrines: '[The Church] is a human construction really . . . A lot of the doctrines of the Church seemed to be very much the product of a particular age in its thinking . . . The whole notion of revelation began to unravel.' Russell Briggs, an ex-New Church leader, told of his disillusionment when he realised that New

Churches could become as institutionalised and 'moribund' as conventional Churches: 'We started this brand new thing which was going to be the best thing since sliced bread and that began to show the normal weaknesses that any organisation would do. We became institutionalised, like everything – it happens to everything in the end.'

Experience takes priority over beliefs for Boomers. In their formative years inherited cultural and religious 'certainties' were jettisoned in favour of authentically 'living in the present moment'. Inspired by the existentialist call to break free from the crowd, from social conditioning and from the fetters of the past they were to have the courage to live truly free, authentic and autonomous lives. Interest in the transcendent was not abandoned, but institutional religion was written off by many as too staid and fossilised. They wanted something that would fit them, rather than something into which they would have to fit. The search was on for 'direct, inward and present' (Troeltsch 1931:730) self-actualising spiritual experience, probably best described as 'mystical' in nature, whether it be knowing God or getting in touch with one's true self. It was important to free the human spirit from potentially stifling social structures and conventions.

The growth of such phenomena as the Charismatic Renewal Movement, certain New Religious Movements, and New Age spirituality have helped to feed the Boomers' appetite for more immediate and personal spiritual experience. Even where Boomers now belong to mainstream churches, they remain highly alert to the danger of churches merely 'going through the motions' and demand credibility and authenticity in return for their church involvement. As Wade Clark Roof has noted: 'Just showing up and going through the motions is what many boomers abhor about church going ... just going through the motions of religious involvement can easily smack of hypocrisy to a generation that has felt estranged from social institutions and insists upon authenticity and credibility as prerequisites for commitment' (Roof 1993:78).

The premium placed by Boomers on experience underlaid Russell Briggs' leaving and rejection of the church as 'redundant': 'Just as the Jewish Faith was made obsolete by the Church, so the Church will be made obsolete by individual experience,' he claimed. Alison Matthews had concluded that religious experience was more important than orthodox belief and practice on her part:

'It doesn't matter how we pray, so long as we pray from the heart. And it really doesn't matter whether we believe in Jesus, or whether we worship God through Jesus, or through some other ways, so long as it's totally genuine. That's what's important to God ... Following my heart and following God is really what the whole reason for my leaving was about.' She had stopped her church going for the sake of her own personal authenticity. She could have continued attending Mass but 'it wouldn't be completely from the heart, and to me that's not good enough'.

Personal authenticity was also important to Arron Coates, a young Catholic leaver, who rejected the mechanistic nature of much Catholic worship. People were simply conditioned to be there, he claimed: 'Because it's Sunday ... they've got to go to church, so they sit at the back, they mumble through a few things, they give money whenever a basket is passed under their nose, and as soon as [the priest] says, "Go in the name of God", they're out!' Arron appreciated the Sacrament of Confession 'because it's not something that you're ever conditioned to do ... I go to Confession when I really feel I should actually go'.

Deborah Clarke, an ex-Anglican Boomer, spoke of her determination to avoid making the same mistake as her (pre-Boomer) Roman Catholic mother, who, thanks to a convent education, had simply been conditioned into accepting her faith without question and, in the process, had been less than true to herself. As Deborah put it: 'I don't think *she* would [ever] presume to say, "And what about *me* in all of this?" ' One suspects that, were it not for their strong desire for personal authenticity, some church leavers would have found it easier to remain and continue 'going through the motions'. Samuel Hartley left in order to resolve his sense of hypocrisy over leading what he perceived as a 'double life', as a secretly homosexual Catholic: 'Whenever I went into a church and prayed or went to Mass I had this feeling that I was hiding part of myself.' The desire to avoid personal hypocrisy was a frequent motive for our interviewees. In some cases this may be attributable to the dynamics of the leaving process itself, whereby, as we have seen in chapter two, at a certain stage inconsistency between what one is in theory and in actuality is recognised and addressed. The context and strength of this theme in the accounts given by our interviewees does, however, suggest that nowadays cultural changes have put a premium on the avoidance of hypocrisy.

The individual and his or her choices is a central focus for

Boomers. Raised in the 'never had it so good' era, they were brought up in a period of untold affluence and soaring expectations. Children were encouraged to express themselves, with the approval of Dr Spock, and to believe 'that somehow sheer abundance would nurture them' (Roof 1993:43). Relative economic security fostered 'post-materialist' values. Instead of the struggle to survive people could now focus on the well-being of the self and the search for meaning. The virtue of self-denial gave way to the new ethic of self-fulfilment. It was important to 'fulfil one's potential' and to have heightened self-knowledge. Life was for growing as a person and for achieving 'quality of life', often facilitated by various kinds of psychological therapy. The self was not something static and given but something capable of being enriched, if people took proper responsibility for their own self-growth. Providing that people believed in themselves there was almost no limit to what could be achieved. Although the economic optimism of their childhood later gave way to recession and, for many, negative equity, Baby Boomers still place a very high premium on the growth of the self: they prefer churches in which spiritual growth is not an optional extra.

Diversity of choice has been an important feature of the Baby Boomer generation, in consumption, media viewing, and especially lifestyle. Religion is a matter of 'preference' and pluralism is highly valued. 'Pre-packaged' religion is often treated with suspicion. Commentators have coined the term 'pick and mix spirituality' to describe the fluidity of Boomers' allegiances and the way in which they happily select and combine aspects of various religious traditions – maybe a little Celtic spirituality plus a little indigenous American spirituality plus some Gregorian chant.

Our interviewees often spoke of their church going – and church leaving – as a matter of individual choice. Arron Coates told us: 'It's my choice to go, and there's no point in going half-heartedly.' Alison Matthews believed that 'people need to find their own way' to God: 'What works for one person doesn't work for another, and what will lead one person to God will drive another from him . . . People have to find their own paths to God, if that's what they want to do.' Her path had now taken her beyond Christianity and she had made an important discovery: 'I was concerned about whether Catholicism was the right way, or Christianity was the right way to worship God, or whether the Baha'i Faith had all the answers, or whether Buddhism had all the answers, and all these things I was looking into, [but] I've come to the realisation that whatever God is, God is something far greater and far more wise than something that would be at all worried about how we pray to him, or how we love him.'

Ex-New Church Boomer, Matthew Williams, told us that his spiritual 'pilgrimage' similarly no longer included the 'exclusiveness of the Christian religion': 'I can't believe that God is about making a decision in your life, and those who make the right decision are going to heaven, and those who didn't make the decision are going to hell.' Donald Harper, an ex-Catholic Boomer, spoke of his agnosticism about the God of the Christian tradition, which is only 'one of a number of ways'. He had a 'growing conviction that religion is an expression primarily of the *human* search for the Other, God, whatever'. He told us: 'I find no problem about [the notion of] unknowable realities, mysteries, "God" if you want to call it that, but . . . religion [is] more than the Christian religion.'

Whilst 'religion' was frequently a word with negative associations, 'spirituality' was a term that appealed to many of our Boomer and Buster interviewees. 'The trouble with the church,' Peter Kendall claimed, 'is that it . . . nowhere goes to the root of people's deep, deep spirituality. It's not equipped to deal with a new restlessness that people are feeling. It's an end of the millennium restlessness. It's a feeling that the materialism and the way that we've gone in the last thousand years has got to change into a new form of spirituality . . . that relates you to the universe, the cosmos.' Interestingly, given his Boomer background, he now criticised the '60s Revolution' and 'twentieth-century existential philosophy' as too 'person-centred' and 'too much to do with constructing your own realities'. His spiritual search beyond the church had taught him that the human person is 'part of something which is much, much, much, infinitely, much greater than we are individually'.

Leavers tend to use open, questing metaphors to describe their spiritual journey. Deborah Clarke spoke of going on 'a *journey,* a *quest* . . . away from the church'. Others spoke of still being on a *pilgrimage* or a *search.* Alison Matthews claimed: 'I'm still searching, I'm still working towards something.' Spirituality has to do with the immediate and the experiential, the mystical and the immanent, rather than the dryness of organised religion. Peter Kendall described his spirituality as 'a feeling of oneness with the universe, but not with God as a Christian'. Russell Briggs had already, within the charismatic movement, learnt to 'live from the source within'. He told us: 'I [still] believe [that] is where God is. He could be transcendent, but as far as I'm concerned he's immanent, the God within.'

Postmodern 'pick and mix' spirituality was not always acceptable to our interviewees. Suzanne O'Leary in Northern Ireland claimed that having your 'own individual religion' wouldn't 'really work' there. In Northern Ireland a person's religion is also an important badge of cultural identity. Madeleine, one of our other Northern Irish interviewees, was tempted to pick and choose within her Catholicism but concluded that it would be 'very hypocritical'. The value shifts we are describing in this chapter have, not surprisingly, also spawned counter-reactions. Fundamentalist religion and conservative churches have capitalised on people's unwillingness to live with too much uncertainty. Samuel Hartley, a young ex-Catholic, rejoined the church because he was attracted to the 'absolute truth' of Catholicism, in spite of its 'inadequacies'. He found it a 'very joyous experience' to recognise that in his own life 'I had this line drawn, and on one side were the things that weren't OK, and on one side were things that God liked.'

Boomers regard lifestyle as a matter of personal choice and are extremely tolerant of others' different lifestyles. The 'new morality' of the permissive society represented a sea change from the moral values of their parents' generation. Boomers sought independence from the old moral authorities and preferred to make more spontaneous and intuitive decisions about the way they led their lives. It is true that Boomers have now become somewhat more conservative in their attitudes, but tolerance and respect for difference remain key characteristics (Roof 1993:45), as does the premium placed on individual autonomy.

One of the reasons why some people leave churches is their fear, or their experience, of being rejected because their lifestyle is in some way unconventional. They conclude that such things as having sex outside marriage, taking illegal drugs, or being a practising homosexual or lesbian are incompatible with continued church belonging. As an Anglican vicar we interviewed put it: 'They feel the church isn't the place for them any more, because I think they feel they've broken the rules.' Another Anglican colleague told us of a man who had stopped attending church 'because he'd been involved with another woman, and, while his marriage survived that, he could not face what he felt would be the moral censure of the people in the church'.

For Matthew Williams, his Bohemian, 'quite wild', lifestyle as an art student, in 1977, led to him leaving church: 'somehow there was a contradiction between being an artist and a Christian.' Samuel Hartley, a young gay Catholic leaver, started to distance himself from the church because of his fear of how the church would react were he to 'come out': 'I felt that if I'd gone in there and told people, "This is who I am, and this is what I do", that the powers that be, or the priest, would have said, "Well, sorry, mate, you can't really take communion, you can't do this" and it was easier just not to bother them [and] to go my own way.' He acknowledged, however, that 'it was my own perception – it may not have been the case'. Congregations might be much less judgemental, in practice, than leavers fear.

It is Roman Catholics who are perhaps the most acutely aware of the potential disparity between their own individual morality and that officially sanctioned by their Church. Official – and deeply conservative – Catholic attitudes to such things as artificial birth control, abortion, divorce and promiscuity have not, of course, necessarily led people to leave the church: an increasing number of Catholics simply choose to defy the papal line. Italy and Spain, for instance, currently have the lowest fertility rates ever recorded, which may suggest that Catholic birth-control teaching is being widely ignored there.[2] It has been claimed that the British, by contrast, are more law-abiding and are less likely simply to ignore Church rules they disagree with: 'once they decide the rules are the wrong ones, they tend to decide it would be more honest to leave rather than stay under a cloud of bad faith.'[3] Whether people stay or leave may also depend on the level of tolerance expressed by the social networks to which they belong within the church and by the priests they know. If, for instance, they hear priests admitting that 'the Pope doesn't always get it right', they may feel able to stay and sit light to certain papal pronouncements.

The post-material values of the Baby Boomers made many highly idealistic. The search was on for such things as world peace, social justice, gender equality and ecological harmony. Their spirituality sought to be more holistic, overcoming the outdated dualism between the personal and the social. The exaltation of greed by British society in the 1980s was for many Boomers a dispiriting affair. As they reach mid-life some Boomers have begun to re-evaluate their lives and to recommit themselves to the deepest ideals of their youth. Where they are church goers, Boomers expect their churches to be concerned about wider social and global issues and not to be mere spiritual bolt-holes.

In many respects the so-called 'Me' generation of the Baby Boomers has developed and matured. Preoccupation with self has given way to a greater sense of connectedness with others. Deborah Clarke had recognised the tension between living 'most deeply in yourself' and living 'most deeply in community' and confessed: 'Maybe I'm swinging too hard onto one side at the moment.' Boomers have discovered that commitment to collective organisations, such as churches, can enhance the self and need not stifle it. Genuine self-fulfilment is increasingly recognised as involving 'the cultivation of shared meanings' and 'the sharing of lives' (Roof 1993:246). It has been claimed that Baby Boomers are ' "a generation weighing what commitment means" ... figuring out what to give themselves to and where to place their energies' (Roof 1993:185). They are willing to commit themselves, but this must be on their own terms. Commitment must be good for the self and its growth, as well as involving the giving of themselves.

## Baby Buster values

After the Baby Boomers came the Baby Busters, born between 1961 and 1981 (Ritchie 1995:147), and sometimes called 'Generation X', following Douglas Coupland's book of the same name (Coupland 1992). In some respects Boomers and Busters share similar values, but there are crucial differences, as we shall see. There is an appreciable generation gap between those born before 1961 and those who are younger.

Busters have continued the Boomers' quest for personal fulfilment and autonomy. Where personal morality or religious preference are concerned Busters, like their predecessors, show a high level of tolerance. In a postmodern world traditional authorities, such as the Church, have been relativised and have very little influence on their lives (Wilkinson and Mulgan 1995:29). These are, as Wilkinson and Mulgan have christened them, 'Freedom's Children', concerned not to preserve the past, but to be in control of their present.

Compared with their parents' generation, Busters tend to be less idealistic and much more pragmatic. Many have seen their own family life break down. Raised in a greedy society, they have seen few tangible signs of their parents' earlier idealism. As marketing executive Karen Ritchie puts it: they are 'streetwise, once-burned, pragmatic and suspicious' (Ritchie 1995:25). This is not to suggest that Busters are apathetic. Given the right issue – such as environmentalism or animal rights – Busters can show considerable passion. Unlike their parents, however, they are less sanguine about the likelihood of finding easy solutions to complex problems. They are much more pessimistic about the ability of politics to change anything. Busters prefer to do tangible things, like recycling their rubbish, than to attempt to 'change the world'. Who, in any case, can they trust to make the world a better place? Their parents may have divorced. Education may have failed to give them the prospect of a job. Employers are forever 'downsizing' their work force. Politicians are accused of sleaze.

In their own personal and working lives Busters seek to achieve balance and a sense of perspective. They want neither to be impossibly idealistic nor to be excessively materialistic. They have seen the way their Boomer parents 'sold their souls' and turned their offspring into 'latch-key children', in pursuit of lucrative careers. Theirs is a blend of post-material and material values. Busters work hard, but also expect to play hard. Loyalty to the company is less important than relationships with family and friends.

Television played a major part in the childhood of Baby Busters. This has had at least two main effects. First, over-exposure to TV advertising has made Busters sceptical of 'hype'. They learned, early in their lives, the hard truth that the products eulogised in TV adverts generally fail to live up to expectations. Busters learned never to accept information at face value and to be wary of communicators' ulterior motives. They have become sensitised to hype and hypocrisy and would like more honesty and openness from those in positions of influence. They recognise very quickly when people are trying to manipulate them. It is, for example, counterproductive for salespeople, commercial or religious, to attempt to win them over by appearing to be trendy: 'nothing earns young people's contempt quicker' (Grant 1996:33). Baby Busters prefer not to be treated as a passive audience. Increasingly accustomed to channel-hopping and to surfing the World Wide Web, they expect communication media to be interactive. As Karen Ritchie puts it: 'a new generation awaits the advertising message, with remote control in hand and cynicism in his heart' (Ritchie 1995:128).

Busters are wary of taking the media over-seriously. They are media consumers 'come of age', up-front about their own critical distance, who, for instance, appreciate television programmes such as *Father Ted*, or *The Mrs Merton Show*, or *The Simpsons*, that break the rules of their genres and engage in self-parody.

The second main effect of the Buster generation's considerable exposure to television is more subtle. Given that television is essentially a visual medium, then Busters will have experienced years of over-saturation of the sense of sight by persistent TV watching. As predicted in the 1960s by Marshall McLuhan (1967), this has tended to attenuate people's visual sense and to change 'sense ratios', making touch, taste, smell and, particularly, sound much more important. Marketing expert John Grant has used the term 'Sensorama' to describe today's 'hot, experience-led, intuitive and creative, sensory culture' (Grant 1996:1). Previously, western cultures tended to focus on visual images and the printed word. People tended to think geometrically, in terms of pattern, positioning and order. Now the other senses are predominant and those senses happen to be, by their very nature, much more 'fuzzy'. The world of the Baby Busters is fuzzy, chaotic and increasingly subjective: 'where being your own person and doing your own thing has replaced the "visual" systems of uniform fashions, style tribes, [and] party membership' (Grant 1996:3). It is a world in which people are more likely to say 'I feel that . . .' rather than to develop a reasoned abstract argument. Where people stand is less important than how they feel. Self-expression is set at a high premium. John Grant notes that nowadays in clubs there is no such thing as 'dance steps': 'the way everyone dances now is a very personal self expression – a kind of signature' (Grant 1996:16). Busters increasingly 'dress to express' rather than to impress or copy others. They prefer to 'pick and mix' and to develop their own style rather than simply follow one.

For this generation church leaving is unlikely to be merely a case of teenage rebellion. In fact commentators have concluded that Baby Busters feel a greater closeness to their parents than any other recent generation. Transition to adulthood is 'neither angry nor sudden' (Ritchie 1995:151). Church leaving will have to do with Baby Busters' suspicion of easy answers; their scepticism towards 'hype' and manipulation; their unwillingness to be treated as passive consumers; their hunger to have all their senses satisfied; their desire to 'be their own person', in their own style, rather

than simply to follow the crowd or the dictates of denominational
tradition.

Josephine, a young professional in her mid-thirties, typified
many of these Buster tendencies. She had chosen to stop going to
an Anglican church in central London, which was particularly
beautiful, but where she was expected to be just a passive spectator.
She wanted to participate in the service: 'I mean, I didn't want to
go to a concert piece, I didn't want to go to see a picture in a
museum.' After being drawn towards the more exuberant, participatory style of a charismatic Anglican church, she then became
very uneasy about the degree of manipulation practised by the
leadership there: 'I just began to feel that we were being manipu-
lated.' Her husband, Charles, filled in some of the details: 'One
speaker ... a very powerful ... emotional speaker ... prayed for
Josephine near the end of the meeting. He put his hand on Josephine's head and was calling down the power of the Spirit, "Come
through my hand and fill Josephine", and really building up, and
saying to Josephine, "Can you feel it, can you feel it, can you feel
the power of the Spirit?" And I was thinking, "What am I listening
to here? This is absolute bull. What is this guy going on about?"
And she said, "Well, I just had to say yes, because he was so
forceful." And I thought, "Well, that's what this is all about. I'm
sorry, this is just not real, this is manipulation, it's highly emotive,
and I'm not interested." '

Tina, aged seventeen, one of over thirty Methodist young people
interviewed in Battersea Park during the 1996 Methodist MAYC
National Weekend, echoed Josephine's desire not to be treated as
a passive consumer. 'What might draw her friends who had left
back to church?' she was asked. Tina replied: 'Not a minister
standing up saying, "Don't do this, do (that)." Not just being
talked down to like you're a child, because we are also part of the
church ... I think we should be involved more, and asked what
we feel, and what we think.' We lost count of the number of young
people at Battersea who felt that church leaving was caused by
services not being lively or exciting enough. One of our interviewees, Dave, aged twenty, recommended that the church should
'try and liven up the services a little bit, and change the way it's
put over, because it's very, like, two-tone, it's very same level'. In
other words, this Baby Buster was pleading for all his senses to be
engaged in worship and reacting against what has been called the
'frightful loquacious earnestness of Methodists'.[4] It would be a

mistake, however, to conclude that more lively worship was all these Busters were wanting. They were also keen for their understanding of the underlying meaning of Christianity to be developed. As Julia, aged seventeen, put it: 'Otherwise there'd be no point to it.'

## Listening to the statistics

Our questionnaire respondents were asked to look at a battery of 198 statements and to identify those which best described why

Table 4:  Changing values

| | Left before age of 20 | | Left aged 20 and over | |
| | Born 1945 or after | Born pre 1945 | Born 1945 or after | Born pre 1945 |
| --- | --- | --- | --- | --- |
| • *Personal authenticity* | | | | |
| My church going was hypocritical | 44 | 24 | 27 | 11 |
| I was going to church for the wrong reasons | 49 | 29 | 36 | 23 |
| I wanted to stop pretending to be someone I was not | 27 | 10 | 17 | 13 |
| • *Lifestyle incompatibility* | | | | |
| I felt my lifestyle was not compatible with participation in the church | 52 | 29 | 36 | 24 |
| I was having sex outside marriage | 25 | 2 | 24 | 10 |
| • *Mystical questing spirituality* | | | | |
| I was tired of being told how to behave by the church | 42 | 27 | 32 | 21 |
| I wanted to follow my own spiritual quest, without religious institutions | 45 | 40 | 36 | 24 |
| People have God within them, so churches aren't really necessary | 41 | 38 | 49 | 31 |

there had been a dropping off in their church going. The questionnaire asked a set of twenty-three questions specifically designed
to survey aspects of *changing values*. From this set we have chosen
eight typical questions, reflecting the general spread of responses.
These eight questions reflect three main areas of changing values:
personal authenticity, lifestyle incompatibility and mystical
questing spirituality. In table 4 we separate the respondents into
two categories, depending on whether they left before the age of
twenty or later in life. The figures in each column are percentages
of that category. In this table a second contrast is drawn between
those born before 1945 and those born since the beginning of 1945.

The statistics show that factors concerned with changing values
were consistently more likely to be cited by those people born
since the beginning of 1945. The influence of the cultural changes
that are reflected here persists beyond a person's youth. For people
born after 1 January 1945, even those people who left church after
the age of twenty, are likely to have been influenced by these
*changing values* factors.

## Summary

In this chapter we have explored some of the far-reaching shifts
that have occurred in cultural values over the last four decades.
We have suggested that, rather than losing their faith, leavers may
have adopted a *different* style of faith, less conducive to church
going, in response to these cultural shifts. We have noted that
people born since 1945 tend to be a 'generation of seekers', with a
distinctive set of values: they have an intrinsic tendency to be
suspicious of all institutions, including the Church; they are drawn
to more mystical beliefs; they prioritise experience above belief;
and they tend to 'shop around' widely to satisfy their needs for
personal authenticity and spiritual growth. As we have seen,
church leaving by those born since 1945 can only be fully understood in this context.

# 5 Growing into a Different Stage of Faith

'When I was a child, I spoke like a child, I thought like a child, I reasoned like a child; when I became a man I gave up childish ways', wrote St Paul (1 Corinthians 13:11, RSV). As a person grows older both the *content* of his or her faith and the *form* it takes will tend to change. In this chapter we shall explore some of the implications of these changes and their links with church leaving. The notion that faith involves development and change is by no means a new one. John Wesley, for instance, the founder of the Methodist Church, believed that Christians should grow towards 'perfect holiness'. The spiritual development of Christians should not finish at the point when they are converted or confirmed.

## Faith development

In the last decades a number of models of 'faith development' have been proposed by educationalists. One of the most influential theorists in this field has been James Fowler of Emory University (Fowler 1981). Fowler has attempted to plot the changes tending to occur during a person's faith journey. He has focused especially on the different forms, rather than content, that religious and other kinds of faith can take. As faith develops, Fowler suggests, change will occur in the following aspects: (1) the way people think; (2) their ability to see another's point of view; (3) the way they arrive at moral judgements; (4) the way and extent to which they draw boundaries around their faith community; (5) the way they relate to external 'authorities' and their truth-claims; (6) the way they form their world-view; and (7) the way they understand and respond to symbols. After analysing several hundred in-depth interviews, Fowler concluded that an individual's faith journey could be broadly divided into seven stages, each, in its own right, fully Christian. Each stage follows the previous stage and builds upon it. People cannot skip stages, nor can they successfully enter a stage before they are properly ready for it. As we shall see, there is usually some correlation between people's chronological age and the stage they might be expected to have reached. By no means everyone, however, will necessarily reach the later stages. One of the most accessible summaries of Fowler's stages has been prepared by Jeff Astley for the Church of England report, *How Faith Grows: faith development and Christian education* (General Synod Board of Education 1991:19–35). We shall here be largely using Astley's retitling of Fowler's stages.

Fowler's Stage Zero, *Nursed Faith*, is associated with the first four years of life. Faith, at this stage, involves the growth of the ability to trust.

Stage One, *Impressionistic Faith*, covers the next four years. Children of this age would not be expected to think logically. Their faith is to do with powerful symbols and images, rather than concepts.

Stage Two, *Ordering Faith*, can begin as early as six years old and may end at about twelve years old, although some adults remain in this stage. Children of this age have begun to separate fantasy and reality, but still reason in very literal and concrete terms. Their faith particularly involves identification with the stories of their faith community.

Stage Three, *Conforming Faith*, covers adolescence and beyond. At this stage individuals have developed a new self-awareness, as well as the ability to think abstractly. They are often highly influenced by the opinions of respected teachers, other students, parents or church leaders. Their faith is often tenaciously held, but so far they have not really begun to analyse their faith and to think for themselves.

Stage Four, *Either-Or Faith*, is entered from about eighteen years old. At this stage individuals stand to one side and critically reflect on their faith. They are no longer willing to have a 'second-hand' faith, merely borrowed from influential others. Faith is personally 'owned', but in the process it can become rather too neat. This stage is often associated with leaving home, either literally or metaphorically. For instance, young people may go away to college, get married, or start a new job.

Stage Five, *Inclusive Faith*, is quite rare before the age of thirty. At this stage individuals are much less defensive about their own beliefs and more open to other perspectives on reality. Their faith is to do with living with ambiguity and paradox. Truth is no longer a question of 'either-or', but 'both-and'. Symbols, myths and stories take on a new salience.

Finally, Stage Six, *Universalising Faith*, reached rarely and usually only late in life, is when preoccupation with the self gives way to a sense of mystical unity with all things. Individuals are set free for 'a passionate yet detached spending of the self in love' (Fowler 1992:25).

Fowler's model is not without its critics.[1] It can sound élitist, for few reach the higher stages. Stage six is, in any case, much more speculative and much less empirically grounded than the other stages. It can appear to make faith too much an affair of the head, rather than the heart. It can sound too individualistic, reflecting, maybe, an unconscious Protestant bias on Fowler's part. Christian conversion is not an automatic consequence of faith development.[2] Nevertheless, if it is not interpreted too rigidly, Fowler's model casts some useful light on the journey of faith and helps to identify times at which people will be especially vulnerable to church leaving.

One of the times at which church leaving will tend to occur is when people are in transition between stages. The no man's land between stages three and four is especially traumatic, particularly since it is often associated with leaving home. Many students find themselves propelled into this strange new territory by the unfamiliar and challenging context they discover at university. It is not surprising that many drop out of church going at this time, getting lost, as it were, in the wilderness, for the lack of sensitive but non-intrusive guides. Stephen Poxon, a Methodist student chaplain, has applied Fowler's model in the chaplaincy context. Those in transition need, he suggests, the presence of faith communities, such as appropriate Christian student groups and local churches, which will offer, on the one hand, 'an "authority group" to replace one they have left behind at home' and in which they can feel secure and make friends, and, on the other hand, 'an open environment . . . where [they can] question, study and search for meaning' (Poxon 1995:73) and discover faith 'first-hand'.

Of course many will already have left church before they go away to college. A peak time for leaving is at the onset of adolescence, when stage two is being left behind. Those in stage two love to belong, to clubs and groups of all sorts. By contrast, those in stage three are more interested in 'interpersonal relationships'

(General Synod Board of Education 1991:23), particularly, one might add, with the opposite sex!

In most churches there will be a variety of faith stages represented in the congregation, up to and including stage five. If individuals feel out of place in a congregation because their own faith stage is lower or higher than the predominant stage within that congregation, this can motivate them to leave. This may be reinforced by criticism from other church members. A stage three church, for example, may well fail to understand a stage five person and stereotype him or her as 'too liberal'. The picture can be further complicated if clergy happen to be at stages three or four and need to relate to those at, or approaching, stage five. At either of these earlier stages clergy may not allow for the validity of viewpoints different from their own.

There will be times when people choose to have a break, if only temporarily, from their church going. Sometimes this is because they feel stifled in their faith development by a church that expects too little – or in some cases too much – growth on their part. Sometimes it is the very stage they have reached that does not sit quite so easily with church going. Stage four, for instance, often involves a critical distancing from the worshipping community. *The Tablet* noted in 1995 that 'many mature Catholics will have been through a period of distancing, even of outright rejection, at an earlier stage in their lives'.[3] This is equally true of those in other Churches.

## Post-Evangelicals

One particular group of people prone to drop out of their churches, or, in some cases, out of Christianity altogether, are the so-called Post-Evangelicals – a term coined recently for people who feel stifled by evangelical churches and who are tired of being told by their churches what to do and what not to do. Dave Tomlinson, a former national leader among the New Churches and now an Anglican, has written a best-selling paperback, *The Post-Evangelical*, highlighting some of their experiences. Evangelicalism is, he suggests, 'supremely good at introducing people to faith in Christ, but distinctly unhelpful when it comes to the matter of progressing into a more "grown up" experience of faith' (Tomlinson 1995:3). He refers to the four stages of spiritual growth identified by Peck (1990), which he terms respectively *Self obsessed, Conformist, Individualist* and *Integrated*. Many post-evangelicals appear to be moving from stage two to stage three and 'outgrowing' their churches, or, in some cases, regressing to stage one (Tomlinson 1995:50). There are important parallels here with Fowler's stages, especially movement, in his case, between stages three and four, *Conforming* and *Either-Or* Faith. Tomlinson concludes that evangelicalism cannot easily accommodate people who have progressed beyond stage two in Peck's model, because the environment it offers is too dogmatic. 'There is [a] high level of expected conformist thinking and behaving – without which one quite quickly feels marginalised.'[4]

The other important factor underlying post-evangelicalism is the influence of postmodernism, with its radical questioning and relativising of Christian faith and other 'grand narratives' of our culture. Tomlinson complains that evangelical churches always believe they have a monopoly on the truth: 'post-evangelicals object to this sense of certainty; they believe in divine truth, but hold that there are virtually no human certainties'. The word of God, for instance, cannot escape being mediated by the 'inherent ambiguities of human language'.[5] In the new context of postmodernity people are suspicious of prepackaged grand theological schemes. 'Post-evangelicals are more at ease with a meccano set which still has a basic set of components but which offers you an instruction book full of different possible models which can be constructed – some more basic and others highly elaborate' (Tomlinson 1995:82). Postmodern post-evangelicals are not impressed, Tomlinson claims, by the 'personality jostling, political manoeuvrings and empire-building' of ' "bigger", "better" and "more powerful" ' churches (Tomlinson 1995:144–5). They long for a 'fresh sense of spirituality' and are turning to the more symbolic and contemplative traditions of Christianity (Tomlinson 1995:10).

*The Post-Evangelical* has been criticised for its neglect of the complexities and varieties of modern evangelicalism. Alister McGrath notes that 'the demand for unquestioning obedience [is] found in some – but most emphatically not all – evangelical circles'. McGrath reckons that the book is 'best seen as an expression of discontent rather than a sustainable and plausible positive proposal (for engaging with postmodernity)'.[6] Tomlinson's book is however less an intellectual debate with postmodernism and more a popular critique of what he sees as the over-parental, infantilising nature of evangelicalism. 'The reason for many people dropping out of evangelical churches is their dislike of the Parentalism which dictates exactly what they should believe and how they should behave', he concludes (Tomlinson 1995:54). He is a sympathetic critic, who says his aim is not to create *ex*-evangelicals, rather to 'take as given many of the assumptions of evangelical faith, while at the same time moving beyond its perceived limitations' (Tomlinson 1995:7).

One of the practical ways in which Tomlinson has enabled some post-evangelicals to stay with their churches and offered them a 'symbol of hope' has been to draw together an 'alternative church' called Holy Joe's, meeting on a Tuesday night in a south London pub. Here, in a relaxed and supportive environment, people can smoke and drink, there are no sermons or hymns, people can vent their anger and the group itself decides what it wants to discuss.

Anne Townsend, who is a doctor, psychotherapist and non-stipendiary Anglican priest, has given a memorable account of how she became a post-evangelical, or, more accurately perhaps, a former evangelical.[7] The trigger was the death of five friends and seven of their pre-school children in a road accident in Thailand twenty years ago. It was as she unsuccessfully tried to come to terms with this tragedy that she became aware of the shortcomings of her fundamentalism. 'The implications of the deaths of my friends gnawed relentlessly within me. How could I believe in the kind of God I was proclaiming ... (one who cared specially for those of us who were his special born-again ones, and who would never allow us to be harmed) when God had not prevented the terrible accident which killed my friends?' Eventually, after an abortive attempt at suicide, to her surprise she found herself in the office of a hospital chaplain who practised as a psychotherapist. He was the last person she would have expected to be of any help, for he was a liberal, of the former Bishop of Durham (David Jenkins) mould. 'Together, he and I talked week in and week out. He allowed me to do what my fundamentalism had forbidden – struggle with doubts in such a way that they led not to death but became the seeds from which new ways of being and believing were conceived.' Since sharing her story, at conferences and in the media, she has found that many former evangelicals have contacted her to tell her how much her account has resonated with their experience. Anne Townsend does not overlook the sense of 'terror, isolation and guilt of moving away from ... familiar religious pathways', but reports: 'I am grateful to have left the spiritual "playpen" in which I barricaded myself away for a large part of my life.'

### Leaving to grow

The church leavers whom we interviewed, from a variety of church backgrounds, sometimes explicitly spoke of their leaving church as important for their own growth. Samuel Hartley, who had left and subsequently returned to the Catholic Church, told us, making use of a footballing metaphor, that he was grateful for his 'great period in the desert, as it were . . . my faith in God and my Church is probably stronger than it would have been if I'd just dribbled along all the way through'. Russell Briggs, ex-New Church leader, described his leaving as liberating: 'Being in the little box called the church is too restricting for me – it restricted my own spirit. To me, God's at work in the world.' For Matthew Williams, another New Church leaver, church itself had been 'a necessary part of growing up', but now he has outgrown his church and 'leaving it is also another part of growing up'.

It would be difficult and a trifle presumptuous to try to categorise our interviewees in terms of the faith stage they had reached. Our interviews were not specifically designed with this focus. There are glimpses, however, from time to time of features probably closely associated with movement between Fowler's stages three and four. In some cases church leaving coincided with the assertion of the individual's autonomy in relation to his or her parents. Justin Wyatt, a young ex-Anglican, told us, 'I think I'd grown up and realised that I had to lead my own life.' Madeleine, an ex-Catholic, explained that previously she had attended church with her parents, but 'now I'm older I've been given the choice, whether to go or not, so that's the reason I don't go very often'. Sharon Chapman, an ex-Methodist, abruptly discovered the opportunity for greater autonomy when her parents announced that they were going to work in Canada, leaving Sharon, aged seventeen, with family friends in Britain: 'I'd had [church] rammed down my throat so much, that I thought now I'm going to live my own life and I really drew away from it.' She would like to return to church going, but confesses, 'I've still got that bit of rebellion in me, "No, you *made* me go." ' Now married, she is still keen to assert her own personal autonomy *vis à vis* her parents. She would certainly never go back to any church where she would be identified primarily by reference to her 'wonderful' parents: 'I'd want to go back under my own accord.' As in the case of the prodigal son, leaving home and church may be a necessary part of growing up and thinking and believing for oneself.

the critical distancing associated with Fowler's stage four was also apparent. Alison Matthews, a young Catholic leaver, told us that, just prior to leaving, she had started to look at her Catholicism 'in a more critical way, in a certainly more questioning way'. Sometimes this critical distancing was associated with exposure to Higher Education. Samuel Hartley spoke of 'the freedom of being at university' and of coming to the conclusion that his views and his Church's views on homosexuality were inconsistent: 'Obviously, [if] they think that, and I think this, then we'd better go our own ways.' For Justine Sullivan, a young ex-evangelical Anglican, it was the experience of taking a university theology course that challenged her evangelical beliefs: 'I think I'd grown up ... I started to question things a lot more and I felt less comfortable with taking what I felt became quite a narrow view of things.' One of our interviewees particularly appreciated the freedom offered by Holy Joe's: 'Anybody can come in there and kind of feel relaxed enough to say what they want to.'

Leavers also spoke of their movement towards a more 'firsthand' faith, another typical feature of those who have moved to Fowler's stage four. Alison Matthews confessed that previously her Catholicism 'had always been so natural ... most of the people I knew were Catholic, a lot of the people I mixed with were very actively Catholic ... and it just hadn't been something I'd ever questioned'. Leaving the church, she told us, gave 'the freedom to discover again my own Christianity, in a newer way'. For Madeleine, a young ex-Catholic, leaving church had stimulated a more personally owned faith: 'It's made me realise what faith I have, because I'd never thought of what it meant to me beforehand. I just naturally went and [did] what others expected of me.' Josephine and Charles Mason, after dropping off from a number of churches, eventually settled happily in an Anglican church. They had recently started a family and spoke of the impetus this had given them to reclaim, as it were, their own childhood values for themselves. 'It's almost like a coming home, a sense of "now we've got to discover these values and explore them for ourselves", and we're finding them again now in the church.' They told us that their church had a good number of 'people who have grown up with the church in their childhood in some form or another, and many of them are rediscovering that again through their family life, that the values that they took in as youngsters are now beginning to have a new meaning for them'. In the Masons' case this movement towards a more 'first-hand' appropriation of their faith was accompanied by their rejection of a highly conformist church.

There were occasionally signs in our interviews of movement to Fowler's stage five. Deborah Clarke, a middle-aged former Anglican, spoke of having moved from 'wanting to intellectually understand to being much more drawn into silence and wondering at the symbols and the metaphysical'. She had been 'caught up in more mystical experiences'. As an Anglican lay reader Deborah had not expected her hearers to agree with her necessarily, she had wanted 'to encourage other people to explore their own spirituality'. Her own religious beliefs had 'changed from thinking of "the old man in the sky", the guy who's in control, to a suffering God, and in quite a sort of human form', but her beliefs remained in process and she described herself as 'on a journey, a quest'. In her case this was currently taking her away from the church, but she relished meeting fellow travellers. There are features here of a stage five faith, which is increasingly open to mystery and paradox, allowing for the validity of the faith journeys of others. Perhaps her church was not quite ready for her?

As we have seen, church leaving is sometimes prompted by a mismatch between the general faith-stage level of a person's church and his or her own faith-stage level, which may be higher, or in some cases, lower. A number of our interviewees told us that they felt stifled by the churches they had left, which had not allowed them to grow. Matthew Williams described his former New Church as an environment within which 'you didn't get anywhere, you didn't dare make your own decisions'. Nicholas White spoke in similar terms about the Baptist church he had left, which, he told us, did not like 'the fact that we had opinions . . . or would speak out if we thought something was wrong'. Josephine and Charles Mason were glad to leave the highly conformist church they had belonged to: 'The pressure is off, that pressure of belonging, doing the right thing, having the right experience has gone, and it's . . . absolutely liberating.' Tim Harvey, a Church of Ireland rector, told us of one of his parishioners who had grown up in a very narrow and authoritarian form of Presbyterianism, only to reject it when he went away to university. When he subsequently came across Anglicanism he returned to church going. A keen gardener, he told the rector: 'Anglicanism is like a trellis and the people are plants. We're not forced in any one way. A good trellis has different types of plants and grows anything.'

In some cases leavers had found that their ex-churches treated them more like children than adults. Sarah Johnson complained that her Anglican church 'used to have a chap there who used to lead the worship, and when it was his turn, if he didn't like the way you'd sung a hymn, he used to stop half way through and make you start again, because you'd got it wrong'. 'We weren't children, for goodness sake', she protested. Nicholas White was unable to tolerate the over-parental style of leadership in his Baptist church, which seemed unable to brook dissent or criticism. He wanted to tell the minister, 'I'm not a twelve-year-old. I have a brain that can actually work through things with you. I will discuss issues of authority with you . . . [let's] be adult about this.' His wife, Kate, a computer analyst, reflecting on their involvement in the church, criticised its childlike worship: 'There's no other aspect of life where you'd go on sitting in a room and doing these strange actions, standing up and sitting down, and singing along with the children, doing the actions in the choruses, and listening to someone, who doesn't really know what they're talking about, talking at you for twenty minutes . . . So why do you have to do that for religion?'

Martyn Evans, a suburban Anglican vicar, described his experi-ence of people at critical moments in their lives – as young adults, as women in mid-life, or when children have grown up – who ask, 'Who am I really?' and suddenly 'want to grow up'. 'People who have been church members decide not to be any more . . . They realise that their faith, even later in life, was actually so childish because of either the way it was taught, or because of a kind of inappropriate dependency which it encouraged on God.' As part and parcel of taking more responsibility for their own lives they decide to shed their 'infantilising faith', together with their church going, at least for the time being.

Churches were not always able to provide the opportunities for growth that leavers wanted. Sarah Johnson found that her Anglican church failed to meet her needs for spiritual growth: 'We needed more teaching. We needed to be learning more. We felt we weren't growing.' The teaching at her confirmation class had been excellent but since then, she told us, 'we were being virtually starved'. 'I did O-level and A-level RE at school and actually learnt an awful lot more about the Bible and the Christian faith at school than I learnt at church!' 'We weren't really living out a Christian life while we were there,' Sarah went on, 'because I think it was basically too easy, we weren't being stretched.' Peter Kendall, a middle-aged ex-Methodist, complained that 'the church is a very, very simple organisation, with a very simple theology [that] nowhere goes to the root of people's deep, deep spirituality'. His disillusionment with the church went hand in hand with a dis-illusionment with its 'simplistic view of spirituality'. As a teenager he was inspired by the ground-breaking book by Bishop John Robinson (1963), *Honest to God*, but was disappointed to find 'no one thinking in those terms' in his church.

Sometimes leavers find themselves 'out of their depth' because they have not yet developed to the level expected of them by their church and they are, as it were, frightened off. One of the young people whom we interviewed spoke of her friend's experience, who could not handle the spiritual intensity of her church: 'I know a lot of people at my church were really deep Christians already, and she was like a beginner, and she felt that she had to rush into it, and she just couldn't do that.' Another youngster suggested that one of the reasons for people dropping out of the church was because 'it was like too much, too strong ... and asking them to do too much, like commit themselves'. As a letter to the *Methodist Recorder* suggested, people can sometimes be scared away by premature exposure to the depths of Christian worship: 'Far too many fringe people are trapped into a Communion service from which there is no escape; many of them do not come again.'[8]

## Listening to the statistics

Our questionnaire respondents were asked to look at a battery of 198 statements and to identify those which best described why there had been a dropping off in their church going. The question-naire asked a set of ten questions specifically designed to survey aspects of *faith development*. From this set we have chosen eight typical questions, reflecting the general spread of responses. In table 5 we separate the respondents into two categories, depending on whether they left before the age of twenty or later in life. The figures in each column are percentages of that category.

The statistics show that factors concerned with faith develop-ment were more likely to be cited by those people who had left before the age of twenty. Nearly four out of every five in this category saw church leaving as an opportunity to exercise their own autonomy. Whilst some people who left before the age of twenty found it difficult to understand the church's teaching,

**Table 5:  Faith development**

|  | Under 20 % | 20 and over % |
|---|---|---|
| I grew up and started making decisions on my own | 79 | 42 |
| The church was no longer helping me to grow | 37 | 23 |
| The church did not give me room to be myself | 30 | 15 |
| I felt spiritually out of my depth | 12 | 12 |
| I felt pressurised to join the church before I was ready | 20 | 7 |
| The church's teaching seemed to go over my head | 17 | 9 |
| The church's teaching was too simplified and unchallenging | 31 | 16 |
| The church's teaching did not give the certainty I was seeking | 24 | 22 |

nearly twice as many found it 'too simplified and unchallenging'. Well over one-quarter of all respondents complained that the church had not been helping them to grow.

## Summary

In this chapter we have been looking at church leaving in the light of faith development theory, choosing to focus on Fowler's seven-stage model. We have seen that sometimes there is a mismatch between the stage of faith development of the leaver and that expected of him or her by the church or even that of the church itself. In some cases leavers have been scared by premature exposure to intense spirituality and have felt out of their depth. Other leavers feel stifled by their church and sense that they are being held back in their faith development. Leaving for them is a profoundly liberating experience – for the time being, at least, their spiritual pilgrimage is taking them outside the church. Leaving is necessary if they are to grow into a more mature, less infantilising form of faith. It may be that, if churches take increasing account of people's need to grow in faith, 'out-growing' the church may one day be followed by 'growing back into' the church.

# 6    Changes and Chances

For those who do attend, church going usually becomes a habit – a good habit, but a habit nonetheless. Like most habits, church going can be disrupted by sudden changes in a person's life. Previous research has suggested that at least a third of church leavers partly attribute their disengagement to 'life changes' and 'contextual' reasons of this sort (Albrecht, Cornwall and Cunningham 1988:68). In this chapter we shall be looking at the impact on church leaving of some of these changes.

There are a number of changes that tend to happen during the course of an individual's life.[1] During *teenage years* there will be the onset of puberty, transition to high school, the challenge of sitting public examinations for the first time and, maybe, departure to higher education. In *early adulthood*, if the economy is in sufficiently good shape, there will be the experience of starting work. For many there will also be marriage, setting up home and the birth of their first child – although not always in that order. Later, in *middle age*, there may be marriage break-up and remarriage, increased job load, job change, retraining, job loss, or even early retirement, the tantrums of teenage children, together with new responsibilities for ageing parents, not to mention the chance of having a mid-life crisis! In *older age* there will be retirement and the need to manage on a reduced income. Energy and health may deteriorate and mobility may be increasingly impaired. Women, in particular, may suffer the death of their partner and become single again, or even remarry. Most individuals will experience at least some of these stressful life changes.

There are other important changes that can come at almost any time in a person's lifetime. The 'changes and chances of this mortal life', as the 1662 Prayer Book describes them, are not necessarily linked to any particular decade of life. Illness and accidental injury can strike at any time. Bereavement, whilst unusual in early life, is similarly unpredictable. Although generally much more within a person's control, moving house and relocation can also take place at any age. Sometimes there are major changes in society that have an impact on church leaving. The substantial deregulation of Sunday trading, for instance, means that Sunday is no longer a 'day of rest' for many individuals.

Why should changes of this sort tend to be associated with church leaving? To begin with, change is disruptive of established routine. If people have had a place for church going in their routine, maybe on a weekly basis, when their habits are overturned by change they may find there is no longer any space in their lives for church attendance. As Martyn Evans, an Anglican vicar, told us: 'It's often struck me how, even for people who are very committed and have been going to church regularly without any question for years, all that's got to happen is that they move house, [or there is] some small change in their personal lives, and the pattern, once broken, is very difficult to pick up again.' They may have been going to church, as it were, on autopilot for many years, but now decide that it is not an essential aspect of their lives. As Steve Bruce has noted: 'inertia is a powerful social force' and change will tend to make for the disengagement of 'those whose commitment is too weak to survive the need for change' (Bruce 1996:90).

Secondly, some of the changes we have itemised inevitably present additional obstacles to people's church attendance. Some of the changes of older age, for instance, tend to make church going less satisfying and, in some cases, completely impractical. Equally, work schedule changes can make Sunday church going very difficult. Thirdly, a number of the changes we have specified are highly stressful events. Some of them are ranked highly by psychologists as major stress-causing factors. According to the scale of stress factors devised by Holmes and Rahe, for instance, 'death of spouse' scores 100 points, 'divorce' 73 points, 'personal injury or illness' 53 points, 'marriage' 50 points, 'fired at work' 47 points, 'addition to family' 39 points, 'change to different line of work' 36 points, and 'change in residence' 20 points (Holmes and Rahe 1967:213–8). Adaptation to such changes involves depletion of a person's nervous and physical energy. The energy he or she will use up in dealing with such changes will tend to siphon off the energy that is required for church participation.

We have begun by looking at some of the common factors that connect experiences of change to church leaving. There are also specific factors associated with particular changes. In the remainder of this chapter we shall be focusing on four key areas of change that have been identified in previous research. To start with, and in greatest detail, we shall explore the impact of moving home on church leaving.

## Moving home

Whenever people move away their religious participation becomes more vulnerable, as the Psalmist well knew when he asked, 'How shall we sing the Lord's song in a foreign land?' (Psalm 137:4). Research by the Gallup Organisation in the United States in 1988 found that 'moving to a new community' was a factor in 22 per cent of cases of church leaving (Gallup 1988:45). It has been suggested that the comparable British figure may be somewhat lower: Michael Fanstone's later British survey, *The Sheep That Got Away*, discovered that moving home was a factor in just 4 per cent of church leaving (Fanstone 1993:63). One possible explanation of the disparity between these two survey results is that church going in Britain, because it is less likely to be motivated by social convention, is somewhat less vulnerable to life change and contextual factors. Another explanation of the disparity is that Fanstone's British survey did not adequately measure this factor, as the findings of our own survey would suggest (reported at the end of this chapter).

Not surprisingly, with the house market having been relatively dormant and negative equity a fact of life for many houseowners, moving home has recently been a less attractive option in Britain than it once was. Some people, however, have little choice over moving. It is estimated that some 250,000 senior managers move around the country to new jobs each year. This usually means their families are uprooted with them and moved to unfamiliar locations (Poore 1992:29).

Most students go away from home to university. Often the course they opt for, or the one that offers them a place, entails living many miles from home, sometimes in a busy urban environment to which they have not been previously accustomed. The relatively unstructured nature of student lifestyle all too easily disrupts established church going habits. As Samuel Hartley, a young Catholic leaver, explained: 'It was just the freedom of being at university, initially, that made me not get involved ... not having to get up

and go to church, which for most people is a grind and a bore.' It
was 'sheer laziness' on his part, he admitted: 'At university, Sunday
morning is not the time to go to church, it's time to sleep!' University chaplaincies frequently offer a regular diet of weekly and daily
services, but relatively few students develop the habit of attending.
As Justine Sullivan, an ex-Anglican, told us: 'Now I would probably value something like that a lot more, because as you get into
routines, especially with having a job, you start to become a lot
more on time, efficient. When you're a student there's still a lot of
room for being quite lazy . . . I had a problem with getting up for
lectures, let alone being holy and going to prayer in the morning!'

Whenever church goers, of any age, move to a new community
it may take them some time to re-establish links with a local
church. To start with, they must hunt around to discover which
churches are available locally, or within convenient travelling distance. They will not necessarily gravitate towards a church of their
own denomination. Denominational loyalty is no longer particularly important nowadays, except to clergy. People 'happen to be'
Methodists, or Anglicans, or members of the United Reformed
Church, but are more committed to their local congregation than
their denomination. They are more likely, therefore, to be looking
for a particular style of church, most often one that is very similar
to that which they have just moved from. So charismatics will seek
out charismatically inclined churches, Anglo-Catholics will look
for 'high churches', and so on. Exceptionally, if they have not
properly fitted into their church back home, they may be looking
for something radically different.

Adrian Dickinson, a Methodist minister, spoke in terms of a
'religious consumer market', in which, according to his experience,
people seek out 'a church thats style of worship and life is similar
to that which they've left, or that which they want [and] link
up to the style of church that [suits] them . . . not automatically by
denominational preference'. If people's search for a new church of
a desired style or location is unsuccessful, their continued church
going becomes rather more precarious. As Arron Coates, a young
ex-Catholic, told us: 'I've just sort of faded out and stopped going.
I don't know if it's because I've moved to a new house, and just
haven't found a church, or if it's just because I've become less
interested.' Alison Matthews, another young ex-Catholic, told us
how 'it was quite a shock to the system really, moving back to [the
big city] . . . and not living very, very close to my place of worship

and being able to pop in any time, day or evening, that I wanted to'.

Even when they locate a suitable church there are, however, other hurdles to negotiate. They will need to overcome any apprehension they may have as a 'newcomer' and summon up the courage to walk into a strange church. 'I didn't go to church, because I didn't dare go to this church, and see all the new people', Tom, a Methodist teenager who had recently moved home, told us. Assimilating into a new church is especially difficult for single or elderly people. As Martyn Evans reflected: 'Maybe because they haven't the excuse of going to family things it's harder for older people or single people to pick up the threads (of church going).' Finding a new church is not always an easy task. As C. Kirk Hadaway (1990:83) has noted, some people tend to 'put this off so long that they become accustomed to having their Sundays free'.

Usually no one from their previous community will know whether they are going to church or not. Research shows how easy it is for members to be lost as they move from one community to another (Bibby 1997:304). Before they moved there may have been social pressure from parents, friends or other church goers to turn up to church regularly. Now those erstwhile social constraints have been lifted and, for some at least, it is like a breath of fresh air. This probably helps to explain why those moving from a rural or small town community into a big city are especially prone to drop out of church going, as they leave behind the range of intimate ties that bond them to their church (Wuthnow and Christiano 1979:271).

Those who are less rooted locally, as a result of occupational and geographical mobility, are more likely to discontinue their church going. 'Cosmopolitans', as they have sometimes been called (Roof 1978), often do not stay within a local community long enough to put down roots. As Justine Sullivan, a young Anglican leaver, told us about her childhood: 'Moving around didn't help. We'd done so much moving around that each time we had to get to know a new congregation, or find "the right church for you", or where you're sort of "meant to be", [and] you lose the continuity that's important in relationships.' Research suggests that it takes at least five years to put down roots in a church (Wuthnow and Christiano 1979:266).

Cosmopolitans may live locally, but their working lives may take them into a regional, national or even global arena. Local commitments, such as to a church, may not be easily integrated into their lives. In any case, as Robert Wuthnow has pointed out, some of those who are constantly on the move, as their career beckons, may prefer to 'protect themselves from the grief of leaving friends behind simply by avoiding deep participation in community organisations in the first place' (Wuthnow and Christiano 1979:274). Others may spend time abroad, in contexts where there is no English-speaking church, and learn to live without church going. As one of our interviewees, Nicholas White, told us: 'We lived in Holland for five years . . . and learnt the lesson, actually you can be a Christian and you can have a relationship with God, and you don't need all those trimmings.'

## Divorce

Marital breakdown and divorce disrupt established routines of church going in a variety of ways. According to the Gallup Organisation's 1988 poll, 6 per cent of United States church leavers claimed that 'divorce or separation' were factors involved in their dropping out (Gallup 1988:45). Sometimes one partner will find it more convenient to move to a different community, symbolising and reinforcing the break that has occurred. Much of what has been said in the previous section will then apply to him or her. Going to church on one's own is, of course, often much more daunting than going as a couple. Those moving to a new area will have an extra challenge, however, to locate a church that is sympathetic to divorcees. They will probably want to avoid a church that is predominantly at Fowler's stage three (see chapter five), for instance, which will be likely to take rather rigid and unyielding attitudes towards divorce. Those who stay within their present church may also feel uncomfortable, especially if they remarry.

Members of conservative Protestant churches who have experienced marital breakdown may find their church going difficult to equate with their Church's hard line on divorce. Roman Catholics will not normally be permitted to receive communion if they have remarried. Even when they do not remarry they may no longer feel comfortable in their church going. Arron Coates told us of his grandmother who 'never set foot in church again after being divorced because she felt it was a shameful state to be in'. Access to the children of the marriage may regularly take place on Sundays, and hence be a further obstacle to church going.

## Work schedule

According to the Gallup Organisation's 1988 poll, 12 per cent of United States church leavers claimed that 'work schedule' was a factor in their stopping church attendance (Gallup 1988:45). In Fanstone's survey 3 per cent of British church leaver respondents specifically cited 'working on Sundays' as a factor underlying their leaving (Fanstone 1993:63). Mounting responsibilities at work tend to compete with church participation. Where companies have been 'downsized', there are fewer people, working longer hours and ever more keen to justify their continued employment. Not surprisingly, people tend to come home from work too late or too tired to get involved in church week-night activities. Even Sunday is no longer privileged time. Some jobs have always involved Sunday shifts, for instance, in nursing and transport. However, many of those who work in the retail trade are now under increasing pressure to commit themselves to Sunday working. Some professionals, now that Sunday is no longer 'ring fenced', tend to drop into the office to get on with their work without the interruptions they have during normal working hours. The affordability of personal computers has also made it much more tempting and practicable to bring work home and to spend Sundays in front of the computer screen.

'It was basically because I got a job on a Sunday morning', Fiona, a Methodist seventeen-year-old, told us, when we asked her why she had left church. Hamer Savage, a Methodist minister in Keighley, explained that the membership decline in his local church was partly attributable to Sunday working: 'We have two regular worshippers who are managers of Co-op stores and they now have to work on Sundays and cannot attend.'[2] Adrian Dickinson, also a Methodist minister, with experience of university chaplaincy, told us that Sunday working was rapidly becoming an economic necessity for students: 'The freezing of grants, and then the reduction of grants over three years, [means] students depending on [student] loans, but also increasingly seeking part-time work to finance their way through college ... I suspect that, with the growth of opportunities for Sunday work, a lot of students will have taken that.' He suggested that this might help to account for the 'colossal membership loss' of just over 19 per cent of under-twenty-five-year-olds from the Methodist Church between 1992 and 1995.

## Illness or old age

According to the Gallup Organisation's 1988 poll, 4 per cent of United States church leavers claimed that 'poor health' was a factor in their dropping out. Those over fifty years old were, however, much more likely to give this as a reason. Similarly, 4 per cent of Fanstone's British respondents cited 'sickness or old age' as a factor involved in their dropping off from church going. Ill health is one of the most important factors that impedes church participation amongst the elderly. Declining health can bring hearing and eye-sight problems which make their church going less satisfying. Mobility difficulties, coupled with lack of suitable transport, can make church going very difficult, if not impossible. It would be wrong to conclude that people in the third or fourth age simply drop out of church because at their time of life they are, as it were, 'disengaging' from wider society. Research suggests that they still wish to participate in church and may tenaciously try to continue their involvement but, for some, poor health, aggravated by lack of transport and poor weather, is an insuperable obstacle (Ainlay, Singleton and Swigert 1992:185). One of the Methodist teenagers we interviewed told us that his gran had left the church 'because she couldn't really get there, she wasn't very mobile, and she'd just had a stroke as well', from which she hadn't yet recovered. 'I think she misses it a lot,' he said. 'She tries, but I don't think she can really get there.' Ill health at any age can make it difficult for someone to get to church or to sit through a service and hence tends to disrupt their pattern of church going.

Ill health has its greatest impact on church going in the later decades of a person's life. This is also true of many of the other 'changes and chances' we have identified. Research has confirmed that 'personal contextual' factors of this sort are predominant when over-fifty-four-year-olds cite their reasons for church leaving (Roozen 1980:439). It is difficult to believe, however, that these can be the primary factors affecting church leaving by older people, except in the case of incapacitating illness. In many cases they will have years of church membership behind them. As John R. Butler's survey in the early 1960s concluded: 'The reasons why a person should lapse after such a long membership are complex, but it was clear that they had to be substantial to compensate for the disruption of what was often a life-long pattern of behaviour' (Butler 1966:240).

The influence of these factors may be somewhat more subtle than bald statistics might lead one to believe. The disruption of established routines may in itself be an insufficient reason for church leaving. This may, however, open up the way for other factors to operate. Once church going habits are disrupted, people may become much more conscious of the sheer irrelevance of the church to their lives (Roozen 1980:446). The death of their spouse may not simply alter church going habits, it may also raise overwhelming questions about the goodness or existence of God. In some cases 'changes and chances' factors will be explicitly linked with other kinds of factors. For instance, marriage may also involve partnership with a non church going spouse, whose influence may come to dominate the relationship. Dorothy King, an elderly widow, who had recently returned to church going, told us how she had gone to church regularly until she got married, but then 'gradually dropped off'. She explained: 'My husband was not a church goer . . . He always said he was an atheist . . . I started my children saying prayers, my first one, but then I got self conscious about it, I think because [my husband] didn't believe in it, and then I'm afraid I stopped in the end.'

## Listening to the statistics

Our questionnaire respondents were asked to look at a battery of 198 statements and to identify those which best described why there had been a dropping off in their church going. The questionnaire asked a set of nineteen questions specifically designed to survey aspects of *changes and chances*. From this set we have chosen eight typical questions, reflecting the general spread of responses. In table 6 we separate the respondents into two categories, depending on whether they left before the age of twenty or later in life. The figures in each column are percentages of that category.

The statistics demonstrate that those transitions generally associated with late adolescence, like going away to higher education and leaving home, are more likely to be cited as reasons for ceasing to attend church before the age of twenty than later in life. On the other hand, those transitions generally associated with a later stage

Table 6:   Changes and chances

|                                                          | Under 20 % | 20 and over % |
| -------------------------------------------------------- | ---------- | ------------- |
| I moved home and did not find a church I liked in my new area | 7     | 24            |
| I went away to higher education                          | 26         | 16            |
| I left home                                              | 31         | 24            |
| My marriage broke up                                     | 5          | 8             |
| My work schedule interfered with attendance at church   | 15         | 23            |
| I had to work on Sundays                                 | 16         | 13            |
| I became ill                                             | 5          | 11            |
| I got out of the habit of going to church               | 71         | 71            |

in life, like moving home, becoming involved in a demanding work schedule, or falling ill, are more likely to be cited as reasons for ceasing to attend church at some point after the twentieth birthday. For one in seven of all respondents having to work on Sundays was cited as a reason for ceasing to attend church. Over two-thirds of all respondents reported that, for whatever reason, they had 'got out of the habit of going to church'.

## Summary

In this chapter we have been exploring some of the 'changes and chances' that affect church leaving. The onset of change in a person's life, whether random or associated with a given stage in the life cycle, can all too easily mean losing the habit of church going. The influence of the factors we have identified in this chapter is, however, unpredictable. For some people, they may actually spell a return to church going, breaking, as it were, the habit of *non* church going. When people move home, they can, if they wish, make a new start, without having to explain themselves to their non church going friends, who may now be hundreds of miles away. As C. Kirk Hadaway and Wade Clark Roof (1979:199) reflect: 'Moving, more than anything else, implies a change. For those previously in the church it provides the opportunity to leave, and for those outside the church the move provides the occasion to join.' Similarly, the birth of a child, especially the first, brings immense changes to a family. Whilst the extra responsibilities entailed can leave little time and energy to attend church, this can also be a time when parents return to church, for the sake of their children's religious and moral upbringing. As Andrew Greeley has noted: 'Once you start "taking care" of people, perhaps, you begin implicitly to assume greater responsibility for their "ultimate" welfare' (Greeley 1992:62). One of the Methodist teenagers whom we interviewed told us of her friend who had returned to church going after being faced by serious illness: 'A friend of mine got kidney cancer and she's started going to church now since she's got better, and she found it good support to get over her treatment.' Some people go back to church because they 'need it at some point in their life, if things get difficult', she added, perceptively. The 'changes and chances of this mortal life' are double-edged: they may be an opportunity for church leaving or for church joining and returning. The same things bring people back as well as make them leave.

# 7    Like Parent, Like Child

The foundations of church going – or church leaving – are laid in a person's childhood, during his or her most formative years. Where parents are successful in transmitting faith to their children and are themselves good church going role models, there is much less likelihood that their offspring will drop out of church. As a recent Church of Scotland Report concluded:

> A major cause of the loss of children to the Church and its organisations is in the withdrawal of parents from the Church ... The habits, expectations and patterns of behaviour of children are largely imitative. Adults provide models for their children. In particular, parents give the lead as to what is and what is not important. The evident decline in attendances of adults at public worship, and particularly among younger adults of parenting years, indicates the kind of model being provided in many homes. (Church of Scotland 1995:629)

John Wesley came to similar conclusions in the eighteenth century.

> What will the consequence be ... if family religion be neglected? – If care be not taken of the rising generation ... Is there not a generation arisen ... that know not the Lord ...? Not a few have shaken off all religion, and abandoned themselves to all manner of wickedness ... This may sometimes be the case even of children educated in a pious manner, yet this case is very rare ... The wickedness of the children is generally owing to the fault or neglect of their parents ... 'Train up a child in the way he should go, and when he is old he will not depart from it.'[1]

It has been calculated that the high level of church growth experienced by Baptists in the United States has less to do with evangelism and much more to do with their high birth rate and evident ability to retain their children within the church. In this chapter we shall be exploring some of the processes involved in transmitting, or in some cases failing to transmit, habits of church going to the next generation.

## Social learning theory

Social learning theory suggests that religious behaviour and attitudes are learned by children, chiefly from their parents, along with their language, socially acceptable behaviour, gender roles and the like. Children usually look up to their parents as role models, although other children and teachers can also be important influences on young people's religious attitudes and activities. Religious 'socialisation' is most likely to be successful when parents are committed to their religion, when they make a conscious effort to inspire religious values in their children, and when the relationship between the child and his or her parents is good. People brought up in a religious family learn to be part of a religious subculture, with a particular view of the world and set of moral standards. This is reinforced, in their early years, by constant contact and communication with their parents, as well as exposure to church going and junior church or Sunday school, as well as, in some cases, education at a Church day school. Even if religion in contemporary society is, to a considerable extent, a matter of individual consumer choice, religious choices are heavily influenced by religious consumption patterns laid down early in life.

When the transmission process breaks down or children fail to learn church going from their parents, church leaving becomes much more likely, if, of course, they have ever started to go to church at all. A study by Bruce E. Hunsberger found that church leavers tend to report that 'less emphasis had been placed on religion in their families while they were growing up', than did church remainers. He concluded that 'the home religious environment may well play an important part in the [church leaving] process, such that weaker emphasis on religion and religious practices is related to a greater probability of [church leaving] later in life' (Hunsberger 1983:34).

A national survey conducted in the United States in 1988 discovered several factors that were important in predicting people's religious activity level, including the degree of religious involvement and church attendance on the part of their parents, and, most crucial of all, 'whether or not one's family usually said grace or

thanks to God before meals at home' (Hadaway 1990:94). Saying
grace before meals is perhaps more common amongst Christians
in North America than in Britain, but it is a measure of how
seriously religion is taken in the home. As church leaving theorist,
C. Kirk Hadaway (1990:94), has pointed out, 'unfortunately, many
Christian parents are failing to provide a clear religious example
for their children'. Social learning theory has drawn our attention
to the importance of role models, especially parents, for children's
learning. Hadaway complains that, 'religious activity is being triv-
ialised by adults in many churches, and our children are watching'.
'What sort of lessons are children learning in your home and in
your church?' he asks. 'Are they learning that a relationship with
God is the most important thing in your life, or that you should
think about God for only one hour a week – and not at all during
the summer?' (Hadaway 1990:95).

The Church of Scotland Report (1995), already mentioned, points
out that Sunday schools, meeting alongside main church worship,
may have blunted parents' perception 'of their own roles as significant adults in *taking* their children to church and of the
importance of being with them in the service and of worshipping
together with them as equals before God' (p. 629). In particular,
the report highlights the dearth of male parents as role models in
the church, church going being a predominantly female occu-
pation: 'the "absentee father" syndrome has become a fact of
modern church life and is bound to send a signal to children about
the nature of church and the religious life' (p. 629).

Our interviewees sometimes gave the impression that their
parents had not been particularly good role models of church
going. Justine Sullivan, a young ex-Anglican, told us: 'I was
brought up to go to church. However, my parents would take me
along and not always stay. They would take me to Sunday school,
and then they would come and pick me up, or I would [just] go
with friends.' When she was ten years old her mother left home
and her parents subsequently divorced. From then on she lacked
a female religious role model within the family, because she lived
with her father. He, however, began to take his responsibility for
her religious upbringing much more seriously: 'I was the child
that he had to look after, and religion became a big part of it.' As
we shall see later, perhaps he went on to overcompensate for his
earlier laxity.

Arron Coates, a young Catholic leaver, acknowledged that his parents 'weren't really very strongly committed'. 'It sort of went through phases,' he told us, 'where for six months we'd go every week, and then not go for a few months, then, come Easter or Christmas, we'd start going again, or somebody died, and we'd think, "Blimey, we'd better start going to church again". So it wasn't like we went consistently every week for my upbringing.' Arron reflected that his own church leaving may have been prompted by the fact that his father had drastically reduced his church going: 'I'm not sure if maybe me coming into this phase is just something that I've picked up from my dad.' Two tragic deaths in the family, on his father's side, had 'left [them] disorientated and disillusioned', he explained.

## Key factors

Of course children do not always follow in their parents' footsteps. It sometimes remains a mystery why the children of apparently 'good Christian parents' turn away from the church. Researchers have, however, identified certain key factors, many of which are within parents' control. We turn now to look at ten of the factors that make the transmission of church going habits to a new generation less likely to be effective.

### Lack of parental consensus

In a two-parent family, only one parent may choose to go to church. The other may be a non-believer, a non church goer, a member of another Church denomination, or even a member of another faith. In these circumstances children receive mixed messages from their role models. As Sharon Sandomirsky and John Wilson have pointed out: 'the result of this kind of cross-pressure is more likely to lead the child to withdraw from religious commitments altogether than it is to lead the child to choose one parent's religion over the other' (Sandomirsky and Wilson 1990:1215). He or she cannot please both parents at once by his or her church going.

A young black Methodist leaver whom we interviewed, Rosabel Abass, told us that her father was the church goer in her family. Her mother went only 'on special occasions'. 'I wouldn't say that she wouldn't mind going every Sunday, but it's just that she never has got up with my Dad on a Sunday and gone to church on a regular basis,' she explained. In Arron Coates' family his father was an active Catholic but his mother wasn't 'really anything'. 'She went to an Anglican school, had Anglican parents, but didn't ever go to church. She goes with my dad really, so she goes to a Catholic church, but she has never been "Catholic",' Arron told us.

Deborah Clarke, a middle-aged Anglican leaver, also had mixed messages from her parents. Her mother was a non-practising Catholic and her father was a Methodist, a 'son of the manse', turned Anglican. She told us that she thought 'he took up with the Anglican church' because of her own interest in attending Sunday school, when she was aged eight. 'My mother didn't, and I wasn't baptised,' she added. As she has grown older she seems to have identified more strongly with her mother. She has now emulated her mother's church leaving and is determined to go one step further than her mother, who, although she had dropped out of church, had 'never felt that she could question [her faith]'.

## Parental distance

Sometimes there is a lack of emotional closeness between parents and their children. Bonding between parent and child may, for one reason or another, have failed to materialise. Sometimes divorce, and loss of custody, creates distance between parent and child. Where emotional closeness is lacking there will be little incentive on the part of the parent to try to shape the child's religious choices, because the outcome is of little personal consequence to the parent. Equally, children who do not feel close to their parents will be less likely to want to go to church to make their parents happy and will be much more likely to leave church in order to spite them.

Sharon Chapman, a newly married ex-Methodist, spoke to us of her closeness to her brother, but not to her parents, who had given her an ultra-strict religious upbringing. 'It was a lifestyle. I can see they really enjoyed it. They could not see that I didn't; that's what was so hard, they couldn't see it!' she complained. They had tended to favouritise her brother, who had 'been in and out of hospital right since he was a baby . . . he was the "blue-eyed boy" '. Nowadays her parents live two hours' car journey away. She keeps in touch by phone each weekend and they visit each other three or four times a year. Their visits, however, are somewhat stilted. It's as if they belong to 'another planet'. They have no interests outside the church: 'they want to see their children, but after about half an hour to an hour they don't know what to talk about.' She still feels considerable resentment against them. Her interview ended with the words: 'the actual church did not drive me away, it was *my parents!*'

## Conflict with parents

Where there is persistent disagreement or conflict between parents and their children, church leaving may be a means of getting back at parents or, at least, for children to flex their muscles and assert their own identity (Sherkat and Wilson 1995:999). This is particularly symptomatic of conflict between parents and their teenage children. There is no point, at this stage, in simply going to church to please parents, because this will not guarantee an easier life at home, as it might have once: relationships have already broken down between child and parents.

Gareth Wilkinson, in his mid forties, told us how much he resented having church going 'rammed down [his] throat and imposed on [him]'. 'I think, as a result, I opted out as soon as I could, as a rebellious teenager, and I've probably opted out ever since, for those reasons,' he explained. Sharon Chapman highlighted some of the issues over which she had conflicted, as a teenager, with her parents. She had wanted to attend a church youth club on a Thursday evening, which used to finish at eleven o'clock. Her parents had been unwilling to relax their rule that she must always be home by ten o'clock: 'I used to say to my mum and dad, "Look, they'll run me home . . . so that you're not worried about me walking round the corner." ' Faced with her parents' intransigence, she would say, 'I've got my own life to lead, it doesn't mean I'm drawing away from the church just because I'm staying up till eleven o'clock', but, as soon as she said anything, came the reaction, 'Don't be disrespectful, you don't understand.' She would plead with her parents, 'Oh, let me stay for [youth club]', but 'in the end [she] just gave up – I thought, "they're *not* going to see!" ' Several ministers tried to persuade her parents to adopt a less restrictive parenting regime, but to no avail. Interestingly, Rosabel Abass' minister had to do the same, because her family was so over-protective towards their only daughter. She was 'cooped up in the house' and only allowed out to school, or to church on Sundays. 'I was fifteen and . . . it took the reverend to come to the house and have a word with my dad,' Rosabel told us, 'and he basically said, "Look, you should let her go out and spend an hour with her friends." I just stopped going to church after that. I got a bit of freedom, and then I just didn't feel like going to church any more.'

## Antipathy towards parents

People's religious choices are not made simply in a vacuum, on the basis of what they themselves want. There are other people to take into account, who will be affected by the choices, and who will react positively or negatively to them. The choices that children make will inevitably have an impact on their parents. Where there is pronounced antipathy on the part of children towards their parents they may decide to fly in the face of what their parents would like them to do and choose to leave church. Interestingly, pronounced sympathy towards parents may also affect church leaving. If people who are particularly fond of their parents become less religious for any reason, they may feel duty bound to remain nominally religious for the sake of their parents, to avoid causing them distress. In this case, people will have left *mentally*, but not *physically*. Justin Wyatt, a vicar's son, told us how he kept 'playing the role' of going to church, in spite of his atheism, 'because I didn't want to upset mum and dad'.

## Inconsistent messages

Sometimes the implicit messages conveyed by the way people are treated in a family are at odds with the ostensible message conveyed by parents' religion. Normally each set of messages should reinforce the other, but if the child has been neglected, abused, or simply starved of love, it becomes difficult for him or her to believe in a gospel of love. Conversely, if the child has grown up in a loving home, it is difficult to square certain versions of Christianity with that overwhelmingly positive home background. Gerard W. Hughes (1985:34) in his book *God of Surprises*, tells of his experience as a university chaplain. He would often talk with people who had given up their Catholicism or were on the verge of doing so. A common factor, he noticed, was their image of God.

God was a family relative, much admired by mum and dad,

who described him as very loving, a great friend of the family, very powerful and interested in all of us. Eventually we were taken to visit 'Good old uncle George'. He lives in a formidable mansion, is bearded, gruff and threatening. We cannot share our parents' professed admiration for this jewel in the family. At the end of the visit, uncle George turns to address us. 'Now listen, dear', he begins, looking very severe, 'I want to see you here once a week, and if you fail to come, let me just show you what will happen to you.' He then leads us down to the mansion's basement. It is dark, becomes hotter and hotter as we descend, and we begin to hear unearthly screams. In the basement there are steel doors. Uncle George opens one. 'Now look in there, dear', he says. We see a nightmare vision, an array of blazing furnaces with little demons in attendance, who hurl into the blaze those men, women and children who failed to visit uncle George or to act in a way he approved. 'And if you don't visit me, dear, that is where you will most certainly go,' says uncle George. He then takes us upstairs again to meet mum and dad. As we go home, tightly clutching dad with one hand and mum with the other, mum leans over us and says, 'And now don't you love uncle George with all your heart and soul, mind and strength?' And we, loathing the monster, say, 'Yes I do', because to say anything else would be to join the queue at the furnace. At a tender age religious schizophrenia has set in and we keep telling uncle George how much we love him and how good he is and that we want to do only what pleases him. We observe what we are told are his wishes and dare not admit, even to ourselves, that we loathe him.

## Gender

Boys are much less likely to follow in their parents' footsteps. Girls are generally brought up to be more conformist than boys. As Hart M. Nelsen (1981:639) has pointed out: 'Girls, who tend to have close contact with their mothers, are encouraged to be obedient and to exhibit responsibility, while boys are given greater autonomy.' Given that, in our society, religious participation and responsibility for religious nurture tend to be associated with women, rather than men, parents' attempts to inspire religious participation in their offspring tend to be somewhat biassed towards girls. This helps produce 'a basic discontinuity in the familial transmission of religiosity' (Nelsen 1981:639), making male children much more likely to drop out of church.

### Birth order

The first-born, especially a male first-born, usually has a closer relationship with his parents than later-born siblings and is more likely to accept their authority. Similarly, an only child tends to be more dependent on his or her parents and more susceptible to their influence. Later-born children, especially males, tend to be influenced more by their peers and less by their parents. 'Birth order' influences the transmission of religion to children (Nelson 1981:639). Of course, both this factor and the previous factor we identified are accidents of birth and lie beyond people's direct control, except that parents could, in the light of these factors, weight their parenting differently.

### Stage in life

Parental influence over their children tends to tail off somewhat during their teenage years. Those who go away to university are exposed to alternative values and world-views. Teenagers often passionately want to be unlike their parents. Later in life, however, they may revert to treating parents as role models, particularly if they marry and have children of their own. At this, and other stages in life, 'connectedness and emulation are more important . . . than independence and distinctiveness' (Wilson and Sherkat 1994:151).

Whilst adolescence may stimulate church leaving, the advent of a family of one's own may inspire renewed interest in the church.[2] Church going, with his or her children, may fit in with a person's mental model of what it is to be a 'good parent'. In the North American context at least, 'taking the children to church is somewhat like sending them to college – both are obligations . . . that a parent ought to take seriously' (Roof 1993:151). As Barry Johnson, one of Wade Clark Roof's Baby Boomer interviewees, put it: 'even if he was "pissed off" with God, shouldn't his kids know about God?' (Roof 1993:12). 'Children are tremendous missionaries,' one Anglican rector told us, 'very often when [people] have been to

Sunday school and gone to church as children they generally want the same for [their children].'³

Even when church going has had fairly negative associations in their own childhood, parents may still contemplate returning to church for the sake of their children. Rosabel Abass stressed that, if she has children, she would certainly bring them up to go to church: 'I would take my child to church, *definitely*, and, even if I don't go, I would make sure that my child goes at least three times a month. I wouldn't force them or drag them to church like our parents, like my dad did, but I'd make sure that they go to church and go to Sunday school classes, because I really think that every child needs a bit of God in their heart.' Sharon Chapman predicted that if she has children she may well return to church going: 'At some stage we will go. I think if we have children then we'll definitely bring them up [in the Christian faith], and that would maybe be what would take us back.' She was very honest about her fears of repeating the mistakes her parents had made with her own upbringing: 'I'm so scared I'd bring them up the way I was brought up.' Sharon hoped, however, that she had learned from the mistakes of her parents, that she would not force her children to go to church, and 'through the generations bring them back again'.

## Church denomination

Children will always be subject to competing influences, other than those exercised by their parents. Some denominations, such as conservative Churches and the Roman Catholic Church, are more effective than others at insulating children from the rival influences of secular culture. Other denominations, such as liberal Protestant Churches, tend to be more 'culture-affirming' and the boundaries between church and world are weaker.

Denominations also vary according to the degree of importance they attach to the family. For Roman Catholics, church and family belong closely together. Protestants, on the other hand, give priority to faith-bonds, rather than family-bonds. For Protestants, the logic of their faith means that ties and obligations to the faith community are ultimately of more importance than family bonds (Roof and Gesch 1995:63,67). It is more important for people to make up their own mind and come to their own personal faith-decision, than simply to follow the faith of their fathers (and mothers). Sometimes this will be a decision to leave the church altogether.

Church leaving does not necessarily mean that parents have been ineffective in passing on their deepest values to their children. Where the parents' denomination stresses freedom of thought and the importance of allowing children to make up their own minds, children can easily infer that 'religion is unimportant' or that 'particular beliefs don't really matter'. Nonetheless, this is 'not a rejection of familial religion but is (ironically) actually an acceptance of the parents' most basic assumptions' (Hoge, Johnson and Luidens 1993:243).

### Parental over-enthusiasm

With the best will in the world, some parents will be so keen to pass on their faith and church going habits to their children that they will try too hard and provoke the opposite reaction to that intended in their children. Parental influence should ideally be balanced with respect for a child's growing independence and autonomy. Sometimes, however, children feel so pressurised by their parents into church going that they cease the practice at the earliest available opportunity. As one of our teenage interviewees said of a friend: 'He originally went to church because he was forced to by his parents, and then he left when he was given the choice.'

Rosabel Abbas told us: 'If it was [the] case where maybe we weren't forced into going to church every Sunday, I'd probably up to this day still go . . . I can remember just going to church on a Sunday, and not being able to go out like the rest of the kids, unless it was something to do with the church.' One of the reasons why Justine Sullivan left the Anglican Church for a New Religious Movement was the over-assertiveness of her, ex-policeman, father. 'At some points it probably made me want to stay [in the NRM] even more, because he got so angry, and wanted to tell me what to do . . . As children you want to have your own independence, and, if your parents assert themselves like that over you too much, it can make you just angry, and want to do things to go against them for the sake of it, rather than because you actually believe things.'

The most disturbing example we came across of undue parental pressure was in the case of Sharon Chapman. She deeply resented

that, as she put it, 'religion was sort of forced on us, and we could
never get away . . . I was doing it because I *had* to'. Even when the
family went on holiday, 'we had to find all the local churches on
a Sunday . . . and myself and my brother were packed off to all
different Sunday schools, where we didn't know anyone. I didn't
enjoy it at all.' Many of her friends at church were brought up
differently, she told us. 'They wanted to go, and they enjoyed it,
and they still go, some of them. But because I was forced to go I
resented that, and I backed away.' Ultimately her parents' attitude
created what Sharon described as a 'block' to church going and
she determined, 'I'm not going to do anything. I'm not going to
believe. You're trying to force it down my throat.'

## Children of faith

We have explored some of the factors that interfere with the successful transmission of church going habits to new generations.
The children of 'good Christian families' do not necessarily follow
in their parents' footsteps and go to church. It does not follow,
however, that their upbringing has been completely in vain or
that Christian influence is not at all apparent in their personal
relationships, business ethics, donations to charity, voting
behaviour, and the like. The 'children of faith', as Carl Dudley has
observed, have 'absorbed many of the teachings of the church . . .
live by their understanding of Christian morality' and 'insofar as
positive values permeate our society, the mainline churches should
feel that their historic contributions have been well spent' (Dudley
1979:17).

There is evidence that church leaders sometimes fail to
appreciate the importance of the foundations that are laid in the
family for a young person's church going – or church leaving. A
recent Church of Scotland Statistical Survey of their young people
discovered that nearly 50 per cent 'believed their family to have
been the major source of information about Christian faith and
practice'. By contrast, a separate survey of Church of Scotland
ministers found that only 1 per cent thought that the family was
an important source of this kind of information for young people!
(Church of Scotland 1995:618,623–4) It is true that John Finney's
study of adults who had made a recent public profession of faith,
*Finding Faith Today*, discovered that only 6 per cent saw their
parents as a 'main factor' that had brought them to faith (Finney

1992:41). Finney notes, however, that the average age of his respondents was thirty-nine (p. 12), so perceptions may well change as a person grows older. This would be in line with the findings of Hoge, Johnson and Luidens (1993:253), that 'the effects of childhood social learning during childhood and youth apparently wear down under the pressure of later influences'.

## Listening to the statistics

Our questionnaire respondents were asked to look at a battery of 198 statements and to identify those which best described why there had been a dropping off in their church going. The questionnaire asked one question specifically designed to survey aspects of *childhood upbringing*. In table 7 we separate the respondents into two categories, depending on whether they left before the age of twenty or later in life. The figures in each column are percentages of that category.

**Table 7:   Childhood upbringing**

|  | Under 20 % | 20 and over % |
|---|---|---|
| I was made to go to church by my parents and it put me off | 38 | 15 |

The statistics demonstrate that, not surprisingly, people who had been alienated from church going because they had been forced to attend as children, were more likely to have dropped out before the age of twenty. Nearly two-fifths of the people who had ceased to attend church before the age of twenty had been put off church going because their parents had made them attend. At the same time, nearly a sixth of the people who had ceased to attend church after their twentieth birthday attributed their alienation from the church to the fact that their parents had made them attend as children.

## Summary

In this chapter we have been exploring some of the effects of home background on church leaving. For many, church going is first learned in the home during their childhood. The chances of a person leaving church are heightened if church going has not been an important part of either parents' lives. Equally, if there is a lack of closeness between parent and child church leaving will be more likely. Over-emphasis on church going by parents can be counter-productive. Parental over-involvement in church and attempts to force children to attend junior church (Sunday school) or church can be profoundly resented.

# 8    Too High a Cost

If a person is serious about his or her faith, being a Christian is a costly affair. According to Mark's Gospel, Jesus warned his followers: 'if any man would come after me, let him deny himself and take up his cross and follow me' (Mark 8:34). Christians have suffered poverty, stigma, persecution and even martyrdom for their faith. There are also significant costs, at a much more mundane level, involved in belonging to a church. In this chapter we shall be focusing on those who leave when they perceive the costs to be disproportionately high.

## Costs and benefits

Commitment to any organisation, including the church, involves costs in terms of time, energy and money. Churches often expect their members to devote a good deal of their spare time to attending Sunday worship, fellowship meetings, Bible studies, prayer groups, church socials, business meetings, and the like. Members are also expected to find time, in often very busy lives, to do something practical for people in need. Like any organisation, the churches need the energetic involvement of their members to keep the organisation running smoothly: *someone* has to run the junior church; *someone* has to welcome worshippers at the church door; *someone* has to help keep the church clean; and so on.

Although the church is not a profit-making organisation it needs the sustained financial backing of its members to balance its books, to keep its roof in good repair, to pay the clergy, and to enable it to donate to charity. Members are often encouraged to covenant their gifts on a regular basis, or even, in some churches, to give one tenth, a 'tithe', of their disposable income. Belonging to a church can involve substantial financial, physical and emotional investment. Indeed unless there is some kind of cost involved it is probably misleading to talk in terms of a person's *commitment* to the church.

It is a two-way bargain, however, for, in return, members can expect to receive all kinds of benefits. Churches help meet a variety of needs, some spiritual, some much more mundane. They can offer people friendship, enhanced social status, entertainment, church-based clubs and sports activities and, in some cases, a route to a place within a voluntary-aided school for their children (Levitt 1996:55). In particular, churches offer people a context within which to find ultimate meaning and purpose for their lives. Churches help to stimulate people's experience of God and to foster their spiritual growth. The benefits offered by churches are not restricted to this life and this world. As someone once described the Christian life: 'The wages may be poor, but the fringe benefits are great!'

Interestingly, some sociologists of religion have taken such language at face value and have recently begun to use models borrowed from the world of economics to understand the behaviour of churches and 'religious consumers'. One prominent proponent of this approach, Laurence Iannaccone, claims that 'the logic of economics and even its language are powerful tools for the social-scientific study of religion' (Iannaccone 1992:123). In particular, rational choice theory has been adopted as a useful tool. Rational choice theory presupposes that people treat religion in the same way that they treat other objects of choice: they weigh up costs and benefits and act in a way that is intended to maximise their net benefits. Christian 'consumers' weigh up the cost of qualifying for the rewards of Christianity, taking into account the actual costs of leading a Christian life and participating in the Christian Church.

One of the costs involved in attending church is that of foregoing alternative, ostensibly attractive, lifestyles and ways of behaviour. Christian consumers, like any intelligent consumer in a market economy, evaluate both costs and benefits and choose to act in such a way that their net benefits are maximised. This *rational choice* approach, with its roots in social exchange theory, is not universally popular with religious believers. Many find it startling and even offensive, as if religion can be reduced to the status of a soap powder or breakfast cereal. The language of economics seems to be much too pragmatic and prosaic to be able to deal with the profound realities of religion. What room is left for the operation of the Holy Spirit and the experience of God's grace? Nevertheless,

religion is an object of choice and there is some truth in this
approach, providing one does not try to reduce religious participation to economic factors of this kind.

This approach certainly appears to cast light on some church
leaving. As we have seen, commitment to the church will always
involve a degree of cost. If the costs are perceived to be disproportionate to the benefits of involvement, church leaving may
occur. People conclude 'there is nothing in it for me' or, sometimes,
that they are wasting their time supporting a 'lost cause'. Church
leaving is not, however, *bound* to occur in such circumstances,
because issues of 'religious economics' may for some individuals
be secondary to, for instance, strongly ingrained and irresistible
feelings of guilt at the idea of leaving the church.

Where people have been over-involved in the church, a sense of
'burnout' may motivate their church leaving. Research indicates
that people who are burned out typically feel emotionally drained
and exhausted. Their health may well have begun to deteriorate.
They will have begun to treat others as objects, rather than people,
ceasing really to care about them or properly to listen to them.
They may no longer have a sense of satisfaction at their own
achievements, neither may they feel that others are giving them
the recognition they deserve. They feel as if they are giving far
more than they are getting in return and they have become tired
of trying. It feels as if they are 'up against a brick wall' with no
escape route.[1] When burnout has been reached, maybe because of
over-involvement in a leadership role or by virtue of the pressure
of too many conflicting commitments, a person may decide that
the personal costs of remaining in the church outweigh any likely
benefits and church leaving is the best option.

This is particularly so if they believe that others have been hitch-
hiking, or what is termed 'free riding', at their expense. Most
churches, and indeed most voluntary groups, know how difficult
it can be to get people to join the committed core. Many prefer to
remain on the margins as the fickle majority. Most churches rely
on a comparatively small number of enthusiastic individuals who
shoulder most of the work that needs to be done. These are the
so-called 'pillars of the church' who will always volunteer when a
job needs doing. Such people are generous with their time and
energy. The rest are, by comparison, 'free riders', who take more
out than they put in, rather like fare dodgers on public transport.
Fare dodgers are justifiably unpopular. They put up the costs for

everyone else. Were free riders to pay their fares, the law-abiding customer would pay less. Free riders also exist in churches – people who put less in than they get out of church membership. Of course, unlike travellers on public transport, people are allowed to be free riders sometimes in the church. At certain times in their lives, at certain crossroads and crises, people need the support of others and need to receive more than they can give. Free riding can, however, be something people do regularly and habitually. The free rider lets other people contribute at a sacrificial level to the collection. The free rider always has 'a pressing engagement' when volunteers are needed. But the free rider expects the same pastoral attention and support from the church as do more active members.

It is difficult to weed out free riders. One cannot, in a church context, draw up league tables of people's commitment, with a view to embarrassing people into becoming more involved. Christian commitment is not easily quantifiable and such an exercise would be counter-productive. One commonly used solution to the problem of church free riders is to increase the cost of belonging. One might expect, as a general rule, that the more the cost of belonging to a church is increased, the greater tendency there will be for people to drop out. Paradoxically and counter-intuitively, however, researchers have discovered that it is churches that ask too *little* of their members that are most likely to have declining membership. This is because they attract too many free riders. There are simply not enough active members to make membership satisfying. Active members want to be inspired and to have their beliefs reinforced by belonging to a well-supported worshipping community, where all 'pull their weight'. As one commentator put it: 'there can be little less inspiring than attending services in a nearly empty church' (Finke and Stark 1992:253).

Those churches that have, consciously or unconsciously, successfully resolved the problem of free riders have usually done this by increasing the cost of belonging. They do this in two main ways. First, churches may expect their members to adopt a distinctive lifestyle over against the secular world, either ruling out some things that are normal in society at large or requiring things that will be thought of as abnormal outside. For instance, such things as divorce and remarriage, sex before marriage, drinking alcohol or gambling may be ruled out and penalised if they occur. By the same token, members may be expected to engage actively in potentially embarrassing activities such as speaking in tongues or receiving the Toronto Blessing. A distinctive lifestyle of this kind may attract social stigma and, at the very least, one might be considered somewhat old-fashioned or bizarre.

Secondly, churches may raise the cost of belonging by expecting their members to make costly sacrifices for the church. There may be an explicit constantly-emphasised expectation that people will make a heavy investment of their time, energy and money in the activities of their church. By raising the cost of belonging, within manageable limits, in ways such as these, the problem of free riders can be minimised. Costly demands will tend to deter free riders at the point of entry: if the hurdles are too high, and if the thought of stigma and sacrifice is unattractive, they will look elsewhere. As Laurence Iannaccone put it: 'they act like entry fees and thus discourage anyone not seriously interested in "buying" the product' (Iannaccone 1994:1187). In 'strict' churches such as these there is no 'middle ground'. One is either fully committed or not at all.

Raising the cost of belonging tends to filter out free riders, right at the start. For people who do decide to join the church, costly demands bring additional benefits. The more it costs people to do something, the more they will tend to value that activity. Those who do join the church and accept its demands will find themselves in the company of other, equally highly committed members. Their enthusiasm for church-based activities will be that much greater because alternatives have been ruled out. Where members are not expected to visit pubs, for instance, the church social takes on an added attraction! Although the 'costs' of participating in such 'high-cost' churches may be considerable, individual church members are likely to regard their involvement as personally satisfying and 'a good bargain'. In this case, high 'investment' yields high returns. Conversely, if there are too many free riders within a church, the average level of commitment will be depressed and the more active may conclude that they are not receiving enough in return for their investment, and leave.

One can press the language of 'religious economics' too far, but this approach does help to make sense of some of the findings of Dean Kelley (1972), in his book *Why Conservative Churches Are Growing*. Kelley, writing from an American Methodist perspective, attributed the numerical growth of conservative churches, and the decline of more liberal denominations, to the fact that belonging to conservative churches '*costs* something in money . . . time, effort, anguish, involvement or sacrifice' (Kelley 1978:168). Mainstream churches were declining because, he claimed, they asked too little of their members. 'Strong organisations are strict . . . the stricter the stronger' (Kelley 1972:95). This does not necessarily mean that people have left liberal churches in favour of more conservative ones. Church-switching, in this direction at least, has not generally occurred (Bruce 1995a:69).

The growth of conservative churches owes much to their success in retaining their own children within the church (Bruce 1996:88). Children raised in liberal churches, by contrast, are much more likely to go their own way. Kelley's findings have a relevance that extends beyond conservative churches. In fact the book's title is somewhat misleading. He later clarified its meaning, suggesting a better title: ' "Why Strict Churches Are Strong" – whether "liberal" or "conservative" ' (Kelley 1978:167). Growing churches, of what-ever background, were, he claimed, 'serious' about their essential task and, hence, attractive to those seeking religious help. Kelley (1978:171) asked:

> Could not a modern congregation sit down together and search the Scriptures and ask themselves: What is it we are prepared – in obedience to God – to be serious about – if anything? What are we prepared – in obedience to God – to die for – if anything? If nothing, then the air would be cleared, and they would realise that theirs was not really a church but a clubhouse-with-a-steeple, and they could quit pretending to be religious, and everyone would be much relieved, including God, who could then turn her/his attention to more serious devotees.

Once a consensus is reached by a church, about its vision, then this must be strictly 'binding on all members' if that church is to be seen as 'serious' by members and outsiders.

Dennis Campbell, Dean of Duke University Divinity School, complained recently that: 'One of the most serious problems for United Methodism[2] is the perception that there are no theological norms, no bounds beyond which it is impossible to go and still be a Methodist.'[3] He might well have been speaking of many other 'liberal' Churches. The church leaver may well conclude that this 'anything goes' approach betrays a lack of seriousness on the church's part and that their own 'investment' is misplaced. This is not, however, an argument in favour of more conservative theology or morality. It could equally be a challenge to liberal churches to be more serious about their core beliefs and, paradoxically, to be willing to distance themselves from those who want to be more restrictive. The Methodist Church, for instance, stands for the best traditions of liberal, socially committed Christianity. It is a Church that encourages people to think, and to live with mystery, rather than force-feeding them with instant answers. There are plenty of people in contemporary society who are searching for meaning in their lives, suspicious of certainty, but deeply interested in the spiritual dimension. Perhaps the Methodist Church needs to be more serious about being true to its own nature, about exploring new ways of relating to people in their spiritual search, rather than giving in to the temptation to emulate churches which generally take a much more conservative stance.

## Excessive costs

The notion of 'religious economics', which we have been exploring in this chapter, seems to fit the experience of a number of the church leavers whom we interviewed. We turn now to look at some of our own interview data. Some of our interviewees spoke of the inflated demands of the church, which to them appeared not only costly, but excessive. Matthew Williams was offended that the lay leaders in his former church were being exploited: 'They had no power and authority in the church, they just did all the work, these poor people were all rushing around, doing everything.' For Arron Coates, a young ex-Catholic, it was the demands of the church for financial support that he found excessive. As a student, he was well-placed to appreciate the financial stringencies under which many people live. He especially resented extra collections in church for special charities: 'I have a real difficulty with going to church every week and having a different collection plate shoved under your nose ... Sometimes I feel that going to church can get very expensive, that grates me because the Pope's quite a wealthy chap really ... I feel obliged to give, and I shouldn't ... You're sat down and you're told, "Now give us some money", and I think that's difficult for people in this day and age.'

In some cases people reckon that they have become much too involved in their church. Their investment of time and energy has become too draining. Tom Mosley, a suburban Anglican vicar, told us: 'I come across people who, when they move, move out of the church. And I often put that down to the fact that they were flogged to death when they were in church, and it's the only way that they can not end up being burdened again. [They were] heavily involved . . . on the church council, being responsible for something or other, and when they get away, they think, "Oh, I can't take that on again, best not to go near the place!" ' Those who are heavily involved in their church do not necessarily leave, however, because they consider their participation too burdensome. Paul West's lay leadership roles, including spells as Church Treasurer, Deanery Synod representative and Deanery Synod Treasurer, had used up a lot of his time and energy. Sundays and 'perhaps a couple of [week] nights' had been taken up, but this had not been the reason for his leaving. He had enjoyed these roles and confessed that, 'I miss it quite a bit really'. We shall return to Paul's account shortly because, as we shall see, as befits an erstwhile church treasurer, the notion of 'cost' was in fact, in a slightly different way, associated with his leaving.

Sometimes over-involvement in the church is experienced, as it were, vicariously. Children can feel that one, or both, of their parents is too heavily involved at church and that this has affected the quality of their family life adversely. Two of our interviewees expressed considerable resentment at the exaggerated place the church had held in their parents' lives.

The first of these two interviewees, Sharon Chapman, told us that for her parents it was 'a [total] lifestyle'. Her mother's involvement in the Methodist church included going to the women's group one evening per week. Sharon's father was a lay preacher, an organist, and, as a church steward, had regular stewards' meetings to attend each week. They were both members of the church choir, which involved a choir practice one evening per week. Once a month, the house group to which they belonged would meet at their home. Sharon recalled: 'You had to tiptoe about, and go upstairs, and you felt shut out all the time.' When she was asked what she thought her parents' priorities had been, she told us: 'Church first, without a shadow of a doubt.' She felt that she had personally borne some of the costs of her parents' over-involvement in the church. Her parents had decided to move home in order to be closer to the church. Sharon, however, in her O-level year at school, now found she had to leave for school at 7 a.m. and the journey entailed three trains and a bus. She changed schools, succeeded in getting her O-levels, but dropped out of school part-way into her A-level course. Sharon felt that her career prospects had been blighted by her parents' prioritisation of the church: 'And I think that was the final straw. I thought, "No, the reason we've moved is because of the church" ... The church maybe stopped me doing what I wanted to do, that's why I left the church.'

The second of these two interviewees, Gareth Wilkinson, another Methodist leaver, told us of his parents' heavy involvement in their church during his childhood. His father was a Scout leader and a church trustee. His mother belonged to the badminton club. They would together attend 'all manner of social and prayer meetings'. His parents would help prepare for the 'big set pieces in the church year ... like Harvest Festival, or the Church Fête, or the Church Flower Festival, or the Carol Service'. 'The church was a very big part of their lives,' Gareth complained, 'I can recall spending an awful lot of time at the church premises in my early years.' He remembers the resentment he felt at having to go to Sunday school: 'I can remember thinking did I really want to be there? Initially because I didn't want to be there all day: because we would get up and have breakfast and go to church, go home and have lunch, go back to church, and so on, and so on.' His time was not his own. As Gareth put it: 'It had to be invested, and it wasn't my choice to invest it.' Both Gareth and Sharon felt, in their own ways, that their parents' church involvement had been, as far as it impinged on them, too costly.

The problem of 'free riders' was acknowledged by Tom Mosley, one of our clergy interviewees. He recognised that churches like his own, with 'a fairly inclusive view of membership', were less successful at attracting and retaining members than churches with 'strict boundaries about whether you're in or out' and where people reason, 'If I'm in [and] if it's hard to get into, it must be worth getting into.' 'Because we let everyone in, [people] think it's not worth making the effort', he said. He wanted people to attend church not merely for what they could receive, but also for the sake of what they could bring to others. A new culture was needed. 'If we don't want people to leave,' he told us, 'one of the biggest lessons we have to learn is that if I wake up on Sunday mornings and don't feel like going to church, then that's OK, but the other people there need me to be there, so if I'm not going to go for my sake, I'm going to go for theirs ... I think that's really at the heart of the Gospel, to have sacrificial love, and that we support each other by those sacrifices.'

One of the factors in Paul West's leaving the church was his sense that some opponents of women's ordination were free riding at his expense and not prepared to make personal sacrifices. He felt strongly that Anglican priests who had left the Church because of their opposition to women priests should not have been compensated: 'I think that if they wanted to go, they should have gone without a penny ... I don't see why they should have been paid at all ... if they felt that strongly about it. People died for their faith years ago, so [I cannot see] why they can't give up money to go to the Catholic Church. Why should we pay for their conscience?'

Whatever the degree of their involvement, people sometimes choose to leave church because they seem to be getting too little in return. As one teenage interviewee put it: 'My friends don't go any more, because they think it's a waste of time.' Others told us: 'They don't really think there's anything in it for them ... They just don't feel the church has anything to offer them ... everyone thinks it's dying!' For these young leavers, church going appears to offer few benefits, making the costs hardly worthwhile. 'We've wasted our time for the past seventeen years', one couple told Tom Mosley, as they left his church. Arron Coates found himself questioning his faith and church involvement, because of the birth of stillborn twins to his cousin's wife: 'He's maintained his faith, and probably shouldn't have ... because he's really had nothing back for it.'

Other interviewees also spoke of the failure on the part of their former churches to deliver the goods they were looking for. Sarah Johnson told us: 'That church, the Church of England, there, didn't offer us what we were seeking and what we really needed ... We needed more teaching ... We weren't being stretched.' Karl Osborne, a suburban Anglican vicar, suggested to us that many people these days expect the church's worship to provide 'spiritual uplift': 'They're expecting to walk out of church feeling better in some way ... And if they don't, if they go and don't feel uplifted, or don't feel spiritually moved ... they think why bother?' 'Is it surprising that [under twenty-six-year-olds] don't join us', asked a letter to the *Methodist Recorder*, 'when there is little in our worship that meets their needs, spiritual or cultural?'[4] Ultimately, when they are not getting the return they expect from their investment of time, energy and money in the church, people are likely to leave, especially if they see the prospect of larger benefits elsewhere. As Justin Wyatt, a young Anglican leaver, explained: 'If I got to spend time with people, or go for a walk, I found it much more productive ... The only benefit that came [from church going] was that mum and dad stayed off my back for it.'

## Listening to the statistics

Our questionnaire respondents were asked to look at a battery of 198 statements and to identify those which best described why there had been a dropping off in their church going. The questionnaire asked a set of sixteen questions specifically designed to survey aspects of *the cost of belonging*. From this set we have chosen eight typical questions, reflecting the general spread of responses. In table 8 we separate the respondents into two categories, depending on whether they left before the age of twenty or later in life. The figures in each column are percentages of that category.

The statistics show that factors concerned with the cost of

**Table 8:  Cost of belonging**

|  | Under 20 % | 20 and over % |
|---|---|---|
| There was nothing in it for me | 41 | 23 |
| The church did not meet my needs | 50 | 36 |
| The church was making increasing demands on my time | 6 | 6 |
| The church was making increasing demands on my money | 3 | 5 |
| My participation in church had become a chore, with little enjoyment | 51 | 31 |
| The church was a 'lost cause' not worth being associated with | 21 | 8 |
| It was not worth staying because it didn't matter what people believed or did | 20 | 10 |
| The church lacked a sense of purpose and vision | 29 | 28 |

belonging were more likely to be cited by those people who had
left before the age of twenty. Half of the respondents who had left
before the age of twenty cited as a reason for leaving the view that
the church did not meet their needs. Over two-fifths in this category had perceived church participation in instrumental terms and
had concluded that 'there was nothing in it' for them. Over a
quarter of all respondents complained that their church had 'lacked
a sense of purpose and vision'. One in seventeen of all respondents
had left because the church was making increasing demands on
their time.

## Summary

In this chapter we have seen that commitment to any organisation,
including the church, involves costs in terms of time, energy and
money. Where these are disproportionate to the benefits of involvement, church leaving may occur. Rational choice theory suggests
that religious 'consumers' will tend to want to maximise their net
benefits. Where people have been over-involved in the church,
a sense of 'burnout' may motivate their church leaving. This is
particularly so if they believe that others have been 'free riding' at
their expense. One of the reasons why conservative (or, more precisely, 'strict') churches have grown is that they attract fewer 'free
riders'. By comparison, liberal churches, which erect a much
weaker boundary between church and outside world, are much
more likely to lose members – but that is not a theological argument
for one or other type of church! People are most likely to bear the
costs of belonging to a church – whether liberal or conservative –
if they have a sense that the church is serious about its task.

# 9 'Tread softly, for you tread on my dreams'[1]

Churches are in the business of raising people's expectations, and inspiring hunger for 'life in all its fullness' (John 10:10, NEB). Many church goers may have high hopes for their church involvement. This, after all, is not just like any other human club or organisation; it is supposed to be Christ's Body on earth. Church goers believe they can afford to be idealistic, because this is the one organisation that can deliver. They may never have verbalised their expectations precisely, but they expect their church to live up to certain ideals. In this chapter we shall be exploring what happens when the reality of the church fails to match up to people's dreams. As we shall see, if people's expectations of the church are not fulfilled, disillusionment may set in and church leaving may occur. In fact one of the reasons why people leave voluntary organisations in general is because they have become disenchanted (Thomas and Finch 1990:2–3).

## Expectations and experience

Sometimes people make their expectations of the church explicit. The Methodist young people who promulgated *Charter '95*, for instance, had a vision of a Church that 'oozes spirituality at every level', that 'takes brave and radical action on social issues', that 'faces dialogue openly and honestly', and 'where God is at the centre'.[2] The signatories to the recent *UK Roman Catholic Declaration* by the Jubilee People, a coalition of radical Catholic groups, called for 'a church that is mature; which accepts responsibility, openly acknowledges and is accountable for wrongdoing and abuses of power; which welcomes all unconditionally rather than causing guilt and fear; which supports, encourages and works for reconciliation and justice in the light of the Gospel'.[3]

Normally, however, people's expectations of the church remain implicit, and only bubble to the surface when, for instance, they are explaining why they have dropped out. Alison Matthews, a young ex-Catholic, told us that she expected her Church to use its wealth for the 'poor and needy' and despaired of the Vatican's attachment to 'power and wealth'. She explained that she shared the vision of the Salvation Army: 'people that really see, as the main focus of their religion and their witness to their belief, caring for the poor and needy like Jesus did'. Justin Wyatt, a young Anglican leaver, spoke in a similar vein about a Church that was not living up to the ideals of its founder, Jesus: 'This character was the greatest socialist there ever was . . . yet the Church seems to have lost its direction on that, and it's become such a money-making organisation, gambling its money on the stock exchange. It claims to have lost all these millions of pounds,[4] but it shouldn't have had all this surplus money in the first place.' Arron Coates, a young ex-Catholic, explicitly derived his expectations of the Church from Scripture: 'Most churches seem to have immense wealth . . . it seems to contradict everything that's in the Bible, that the Church should be so wealthy, and so that is a real problem for me.'

It is not simply that leavers project their own expectations on to the church, although some do. Our interviewees spoke of funda-mental inconsistencies between what the church had led them to expect, in its evangelism and teaching, and the rather more mundane reality of the church as they experienced it. Justin Wyatt complained that 'They spout about giving to others and sharing [but] the congregation is very right wing . . . They'll go home and they'll not do any of it, and it just seems a bit hypocritical!'

Arron Coates, similarly, found the hypocrisy of church goers hard to tolerate. He described one particular prominent family in his childhood parish: 'They all went to this Catholic school and they were always there standing at the door, chests out in their Sunday best, making sure that everybody knew how great Cath-olics they were. And once, I was at a football match, and there was a black player, and there were people shouting, "Get back on your banana boat, you black so-and-so." And it was them, it was the dad and the ten-year-old shouting out really racist abuse. That was on the Saturday, and then on the Sunday they're in church.' Another young Catholic, Suzanne O'Leary, was offended by the 'dreadful hypocrisy' of the Church in trying to cover up child abuse by priests. It was the Church's failure to acknowledge publicly its own inconsistencies that especially concerned her: 'There's no saying, "We're sorry", nothing like that, no repentance.'

Sometimes our interviewees explicitly acknowledged the extent of their expectations of the church. Nicholas and Kate White, who had left a New Church, were particularly distressed to be asked to leave their fellowship: 'I think partly because our expectation had been quite high – it was good, it was fun to get involved.' Ex-New Church leader, Russell Briggs, had believed that his Church was 'God's kingdom on earth', until disillusionment set in and he saw that it was just like any other denomination. Perhaps expectations were sometimes over-inflated. Interestingly, Justine Sullivan, an ex-Anglican, confided that were she ever to return to church she would 'not expect too much from it'.

Where people's expectations of their church are not met they may, instead of leaving, decide to try to reform the church from within, to bring it into line with their own ideals. This can only happen, however, if individuals feel that they are likely to be able to have a significant impact. Anglican vicar, John Ingram, told us of a parishioner who had moved from another church because of a clash of principles: 'I suspect, if a similar problem came up [here], he would leave again and go somewhere else on a matter of principle, [saying] "This is not the right way to deal with money, that is not the right thing to spend it on, therefore I shall go. *I have no way of changing it*, so I shall go." ' If people feel powerless to inspire change in their church, they are more likely to leave.

Rigid, authoritarian churches may appear particularly impervious to change. Arron Coates perceived the Catholic Church as 'too stuck in its views' in dealing with such issues as abortion and birth control, 'refusing to have any sort of leeway or any form of discussion ... especially when it comes to young people ... it's driving people away'. In Nicholas White's New Church the leadership expected, as he put it, 'to just lay down the law to people'. He wanted to question the minister's concept of 'worship' music: 'The minister had this peculiar thing, where if you were singing a chorus fast, that was "praise", and if you were singing a chorus slowly that was "worship" ... which to us was a little bizarre, to say the least. [So] the Holy Spirit is about tempo? But, of course, you weren't allowed to say things like that, because then you were criticising the minister!' Sometimes people invest a lot of hope for change in the coming of a new minister who will 'do things differently', only to find their hopes dashed.

Inevitably, churches can never satisfy everyone, all of the time. Some people are inveterate complainers and even a 'perfect church' would fail to impress them. There is, of course, no agreed definition of what a 'perfect church' would look like. People's expectations of the church differ. One Christian's mental model of the ideal church[5] may be radically different from another's. Some, for instance, would expect their church to challenge injustice and inequality in society; others would insist that 'the church should stay out of politics'. Given that people's conceptions of the ideal church differ, any single church is unlikely to please everyone. Many churches find themselves in a state of uneasy equilibrium, satisfying most people, most of the time.

When changes of various kinds happen within churches this is bound to upset some people's expectations. Individuals may leave if they perceive that a substantial shift has occurred from their ideal vision of what the church should be like. As John Ingram put it: 'People change because the musical tradition changes, or because the hymnbook changes ... because their reason for coming, I guess, is that they do things in a particular way. Some folks cope with change very, very badly.' Matthew Williams, a New Church leaver, was disappointed when the worship-style of his church became more inhibited and offered him far less freedom of expression: '[Previously] it was very lively and exciting [with] lots of art and so on. I used to do really weird things. I used to do a handstand in the church, because it was a sort of prophetic sign, and all sorts of things, and they'd like it ... I actually prayed singing. [There was] a shaman-like quality [to] some of the sort of things that I'd get into.' After the influx of people into the church who were 'much less kind of wild', worship services became more restrained 'and that put a dampening on the whole thing'.

Changes in worship style do not necessarily automatically lead a person to leave. Richard Elliott, an elderly Anglican leaver, told us that he disapproved of dancing and hand-clapping, 'which I thought were more suitable for a cabaret than a church service', but emphasised that 'they weren't things on which I was prepared to leave the church ... they weren't important enough'. Karl Osborne, a suburban Anglican vicar, reckoned that people seldom leave church nowadays because of changes of this sort: 'People are used to the church changing: the services have changed, the words have changed, the orders have changed, that's happened ... I think the people for whom the church has "always been like this, and that's how I want it, and I don't want it to change", they've gone already.'

Worship-style changes are, of course, just one of the possible changes that can occur. One of the peak times for change, and hence disaffection, is when a new member of clergy arrives. As Tim Harvey, a Church of Ireland rector, admitted, when he first arrived he was not able to please everyone. One former parishioner was offended by his practice of giving baptismal candles: 'He thought I wasn't a staunch enough Protestant, and he didn't think that I was evangelical enough in my sermons.' Sometimes local churches close down and people are expected to adjust to a different church. As we have seen in chapter six, finding a new 'spiritual home' can be very challenging.

Given that the Church is a human, as well as potentially a divinely inspired, institution it is bound to fall short of its ideals, and to be subject to sociological dynamics that tend to dilute its original aims. John Wesley recognised that, even in his own lifetime, the 'pure religion' of the Methodist movement which he had founded was continually decaying: 'although the form of religion remains, the spirit is swiftly vanishing away.'[6] Deborah Clarke, an Anglican, spoke to us in similar terms about the church which she had left, describing its 'collective attempt to domesticate the spirit', which she found 'horrible, distasteful'. In her experience, church going was less about the mystery of God and more to do with 'people turning and telling you not to sit in that pew because that's where the Brownies sit!'

The difference between church goers and church leavers is, perhaps, that church goers are more willing to forgive their church for becoming like other institutions. Russell Briggs, an ex-New Church Leader, told us that he had gone into the Free Churches, 'found that they weren't "free", and that they were just as moribund as everyone else'. Having given up on Free Churches he had put his hope in New Churches, only to find that they 'show[ed] the normal weaknesses that any organisation would do'. 'We became institutionalised', he complained, and, because this was not something he was prepared to tolerate, he became disillusioned with church *per se*.

In the rest of this chapter we shall be focusing on a number of areas, highlighted by our interviewees, in which expectations of the church were not realised. We shall look at expectations of worship, pastoral care, leadership style and the church's teachings. This will not be an exhaustive list, just a selection of some of the more important potential weak spots.

## Worship

Our interviewees had various expectations of worship, not always compatible with each other. Worship was expected to involve the congregation, to be participatory, to have substance, to be spiritually uplifting and inspiring, to be relevant, to make use of modern media, to be 'alternative', to be lively, to be in tune with modern culture, to be dynamic, to offer a sense of fellowship, to have a certain uniformity week-by-week, to be reverent, to be traditional, to be formal, to have an air of mystery, to be true to modern biblical scholarship, to be offered in a variety of styles. Sometimes it was easier to define worship by what it was *not* expected to be: worship was not to have tambourines and guitars, not to be emotionally manipulative, not to be amateurish, not to be too structured, not to be just a routine, not to be mechanical, not to be nondescript, not to be boring, not to be predictable, not to be old-fashioned.

For most items in the preceding list it would be possible to identify a church goer who wanted exactly the opposite from their church. It so happens that two of our interviewees, Richard Elliott and Sarah Johnson, both left the same Anglican church, but had diametrically opposed expectations of worship. Richard wanted greater uniformity, preferred *The Book of Common Prayer*, and favoured more accent on worship rather than 'fellowship'. Sarah, on the other hand, felt that worship had become too routine: 'It was quite easy to mentally switch off from the words that were coming out of my mouth, when we were saying the Creed . . . and then my mind would be on what the children were doing next to me, or "has the roast turned itself off by now?" ' Her expectation of worship was that it should be less liturgical, less predictable and more 'alive'. When she eventually found a replacement church it was one where she felt 'really welcomed' at worship. Evidently, given such divergent expectations, churches will have a hard time satisfying the demands of all their members!

Worship expectations are, however, much more than simply a matter of differing tastes, and may reflect much deeper considerations. When Anglican Church attendance figures showing alarming rates of decline were published in February 1997 commentators were quick to attribute the Church's difficulties to its espousal of the wrong style of worship. People were simply 'voting with their feet' because they had no taste for 'clappy and happy, huggy-and-feely sorts of worship' which treat God as a 'candy-floss idol ... an ecclesiastical version of a health farm', claimed Lord Runcie, former Archbishop of Canterbury.[7] On the contrary, retorted George Austin, Archdeacon of York, 'evangelical churches are so full that they are "church-planting" '; indeed to decry 'a form of worship which meets the needs of great numbers of folk ... is to be either monstrously arrogant or foolishly blinkered'.[8] Ultimately it was a matter of taste: some people left churches because they had no stomach for modern worship, others were alienated by traditional worship. Such reactions probably fail to reach the heart of the matter.

Theologically authentic worship, rather than that which merely reflects popular culture, is most likely to retain people. As theologian Martyn Percy has perceptively noted:

> Bad Taste ... is not the issue. The key concern (in relation to evangelicalism) is a style of worship which does not offer any real theological basis for individuals to mature in their faith. The danger is that once people have become bored with anodyne and escapist worship they will not move on to a style which allows room for spiritual development. They will simply chuck the whole product away.[9]

Other styles of church also need to take care that their worship does not simply reflect present, or past, culture and to ensure that worshippers are not spiritually short-changed. People, rightly, have high hopes of worship, which, if they are not satisfied, can cause them to switch churches or drop out altogether.

## Pastoral care

Church goers' expectations when it comes to pastoral care are somewhat less varied. Ideally, pastoral care in the Christian context should 'admonish the careless, encourage the faint-hearted, support the weak, and be very patient' (1 Thessalonians 5:14, NEB). It should involve healing, sustaining, guiding and reconciling – 'using our imagination to try to answer others' needs' (Wright 1982:11). When the church fails to live up to these ideals, people may forsake the church that they perceive as having forsaken them.

As Anglican vicar, John Ingram, put it: 'Sometimes the church does not live up to a person's expectations: "nobody visits me; I don't see the Vicar!" '

Sarah Johnson complained to us of accumulated pastoral neglect on the part of her church. She was disenchanted by her church's failure to visit her when she was 'feeling very low' after the birth of one of her children. When her mother, who had been very active in the church, had died, Sarah's 'world [had fallen] apart'. She told us: 'I thought at least the church will uphold my family through this, [but] we didn't get the support, we didn't get help that we needed.' She felt deeply hurt by the fact that, although her father lived just round the corner from the church, he 'never got any support' and received just 'one or two visits in the whole time [of his bereavement] by a couple of people'. She later joined a New Church, which she perceived as offering much better pastoral support. There is always the possibility that she engaged in a measure of 'retrospective reinterpretation', as she compared life 'before' and 'after' her discovery of the New Church. Such churches often encourage their members to think in relatively negative terms about their previous church involvement. Their previous church was part of the 'problem', for which the New Church is the 'solution'. It does, however, appear that real perceptions of pastoral neglect underlay Sarah's church leaving.

In the case of Matthew Williams, who left a New Church, he felt that he was a victim not only of neglect but of pastoral incompetence. He had received what he later perceived to be 'horrific' and 'abusive' counselling from his pastor. Promises of confidentiality had not been kept and his problems had been 'gossiped throughout the whole church'. The counselling had been over-directive, such that it was not until he left that he 'got [his] mind back again'. The pastor had accused him of being gay and of 'being in love with him'. Matthew later realised that his real difficulties were to do with unfinished psychological business relating to the death of his father. He complained that the pastor had jumped to the wrong conclusions, interpreting his dreams about his father as homosexual 'sexual fantasies'. 'It was a misunderstanding of who I am,' Matthew said, angrily. 'I couldn't carry on in the church with this history, which had made me so unhappy for so long.' Ironically, his expectations of the church had been so strong that he had chosen to ignore previous rumours of 'abuse', including 'physical abuse of his wife' on the part of the pastor. When pastoral care is unprofessional, over-directive or simply under-delivered people can become disillusioned with their church involvement.

## Leadership style

Sometimes people feel let down by the leadership style of their church. Church goers have a right to expect that power will be exercised within the Church in a specifically Christian manner, reflecting 'God's domination-free order'. The reign of God, which should be seen in microcosm in the Church, is, as biblical theologian, Walter Wink, has put it: 'characterised by partnership, interdependence, equality of opportunity, and mutual respect . . . this egalitarian realm repudiates violence, domination hierarchies, patriarchy, racism, and authoritarianism' (Wink 1992:107). Where these ideals are insufficiently realised an individual may look elsewhere.

Leavers' concerns are sometimes voiced in quite general terms. As one of the Methodist teenagers whom we interviewed put it: 'Our friends fell out with the people who were running [the church], so that's why they left.' Or as Anglican vicar, Guy Mitelman, described it: 'A number of people leave because they don't get on well with the vicar, or they don't like the way that the parish is being run.'

Others are more specific about their church's leadership style. Many of our interviewees complained of authoritarianism and a lack of democracy. This was mostly within the Roman Catholic Church and New Churches, although Gareth Wilkinson, an ex-Methodist, also described his disillusionment with many of the lay leaders in his church who were 'little Hitlers . . . ill-equipped to be in positions of responsibility and authority'. Donald Harper, a former Catholic priest, felt that, under the present Pope, 'the clock was being set very firmly back' towards a Church with a pyramidical power structure, contradicting the vision of the Second Vatican Council, of which he had been a 'fervent supporter'. Arron Coates resented what he termed the 'dreadful hierarchy' of his Church, centring on the Pope, but also reproduced at parish level, where even the choir 'get to look down on everyone [else]!' However much the Pope claimed to have supreme authority and to speak for God, unless the Church became more egalitarian, 'unless women are seen to be taking a more active role in the decisions of the Church, and are being treated within equal terms in the Church', he would remain unconvinced.

Alison Matthews was similarly angered by the 'power hierarchy' of the Catholic Church which was 'exclusively male and probably always will be' and was unimpressed by token female altar-servers and Scripture-readers. Father Sean Logan, a Catholic priest and youth worker, felt that lay people were under-involved in the leadership of the Church: 'I think that we need to involve our people an awful lot more, because [they] are gifted in far more ways than we even accept or appreciate as priests ... And the sooner we do it, the better for ourselves, [otherwise] we'll have no one left by the time we do!' The structures of the Church were so 'hard and fast' that they 'turn everybody off', added Father Logan. The leadership of the Church was badly in need of people who were more 'open and flexible with their thinking'.

Those who had left New Churches also complained of authoritarian leadership styles. Russell Briggs rejected the practice of 'shepherding' within New Churches, whereby individuals sometimes had a very directive 'spiritual mentor'. 'Submission to these little popes' was, he felt, a 'dehumanising thing'. Kate White had left an authoritarian Baptist church which, she told us, 'was run very much as a sort of hierarchy. The minister was in charge. And in theory he had this team of elders who supported him, and the deacons who supported them. But the practice seemed to be [that] he would say what goes and tell everyone that they had to agree with him.' Kate and her husband, Nicholas, went on to describe their loss of confidence in the minister's humiliating and manipulative leadership style, his untrustworthiness, and his refusal to allow constructive criticism. It was as if 'he could do what he liked, [because] he was a minister'. This was also a patriarchal church in which 'women don't really have a say, as though we're a bit weird', Kate complained. Matthew Williams described an authoritarian power structure in the New Church he had left. Only those at the top of the pyramid had real power. The 'poor deacons ... had loads of responsibility, but they absolutely had [expletive]-all authority really'. Ultimately he had perceived the leadership style to be dictatorial, demeaning, exploitative, lacking in consistency and fear-inducing.

One of the reasons why people forsook the Anglican Sheffield Nine O'Clock Service (NOS) was the alleged power abuse by its leader. NOS achieved notoriety in August 1995 after widely publicised allegations of sexual misconduct on the part of its leader, Anglican clergyman, Chris Brain. Roland Howard has traced the rise of what in theory was a socially committed, ecologically aware congregation, engaging effectively with postmodern image-based culture. The NOS Planetary Mass was 'truly postmodern religious art of the highest order' (Howard 1996:95). However, as Howard documents, in fact, under Brain's abusive leadership, NOS developed into a cult within the Church. Far from being the more open, democratic, non-sexist, alternative community it claimed to be, it was characterised by fear, a guilt-inducing culture, extreme hierarchy, dependency, manipulation, sexism and excessive secrecy. Perhaps the most challenging aspect of Howard's account is his suggestion that abuse of power is not confined to NOS 'but the Church . . . doesn't close churches down if you complain that your leader seems power-crazed and psychologically abuses people . . . of course if it's sex, then they react in 24 hours' (Howard 1996:141).

Conversely, some of our interviewees felt that their churches had been over-democratic, with too little sense of direction from the leadership. Russell Briggs initially left the Church of England because of his disillusionment with 'such a broad church', in which 'there's no such thing as heresy!' and vicars can be as 'eccentric' as they wish. As an evangelical he was disappointed at the clergy's lack of accountability and unwillingness to give a clear theological lead. It has been plausibly suggested that some have switched from Anglicanism to Catholicism because they perceived the Church of England to be too democratic and believed that such 'deep matters' as women's ordination should not have been 'decided in a democratic forum, without reference to traditions of Christendom or divine authority'.[10] Whatever individuals' ideal of the perfect organisational structure for the church happens to be, their expectations may be disappointed and disillusionment may set in.

## The church's teachings

The teachings of their church may also disappoint leavers. Sometimes they complain that it is not clear what their church believes in. Generally, however, they part company over particular teachings, which are, for example, perceived to be too conservative or too liberal, too distinctive or not distinctive enough, too hard-line or too tolerant. Perhaps the most controversial area is that of sexual morality.

Young Catholics, for instance, sometimes find their Church's teachings on sexual morality far too conservative and restrictive. Arron Coates found it hard to believe that having sex outside marriage 'in a loving relationship' was sinful. 'I don't want to be part [of a Church] where I've to continually apologise for something that I don't really feel bad about,' he told us. He also felt that the Church's attitude to contraception and sex education was 'irresponsible', allowing young people to get 'into situations that they're not educated to handle' and within which 'they can't turn to their Church [for help]'. Other young Catholics complained that male celibate priests were not the ideal people to 'preach about contraception and abortion and divorce . . . because they don't have the experience'. An older ex-Catholic, Donald Harper, described the Church's teaching on contraception as 'gravely deformed, in the light of the [over-]population problem'. Wesley Harris, an African ex-Methodist computer analyst in his thirties, complained about what he saw as his Church's 'double standards' over sexual ethics: 'We can ordain homosexual priests, but you guys can't have sex outside of marriage.'

On the other hand, some find their Church's teachings too liberal. For Richard Elliott, an Anglican leaver, it was his Church's 'unscriptural teachings', and 'lack of clear moral teaching' in relation to such matters as homosexuality and divorce, that caused him to leave. 'I can't equate what they're saying with what the Scripture says,' he told us. 'If the Church won't point out that God regards these activities as sinful, nobody else [will].' Richard complained that the Church's philosophy seemed to be 'if you can't beat 'em, join 'em!' and that the Church had 'fudged the issues'. Tom Mosley, an Anglican vicar, told us that he simply could not present the faith in such 'black and white terms': 'My sort of Christianity is based on exploration after truth.' He recognised, however, that 'some people will be put off by that'. Some have switched to the Roman Catholic Church from other Churches precisely because its stance is uncompromising. As novelist Piers Paul Read has put it: 'A lot of people who have led dissolute lives know it in their hearts. They don't want to go to a parson who says: "Don't worry, we don't think that is sinful any more." They want someone to say: "Yes, that is sinful and I am authorised to forgive you." '[11]

Sometimes Churches end up offending both liberals and conservatives. The Methodist Church's debate and Statement on

*Human Sexuality* at its 1993 national Conference, has been regarded as an unsatisfactory compromise both by those who felt it was too radical and those who felt it was not radical enough. As a former Methodist President Leslie Griffiths put it, in commenting on Methodism's declining membership figures: 'the aftermath of the Church's wounding debate . . . has seen an ebbing away of some and the discouragement of others.'[12]

Teaching on sexual morality is, of course, only one aspect of the Church's teaching. Indeed sometimes interviewees felt that there was too much accent placed on the Church's moral teachings. One Methodist teenager told us she did not simply want 'a minister standing up saying, "Don't do that, do this" '; instead he should be 'actually talking about what God's about'. Theological teachings can, however, raise almost as much controversy as moral teachings, as David Jenkins, erstwhile Bishop of Durham, demonstrated!

Whatever style of teaching church goers require, liberal or conservative, they are generally agreed that it needs to be relevant to their situations and to address the issues that are uppermost in their lives. People, especially the young, often complain that the church is 'boring'. Some simply mean that it is not 'entertaining' or 'lively' enough, but others are expressing a hunger for a church that connects with the rest of their lives. If the church's teaching is perceived as unintelligible or irrelevant people are more likely to drop out. One of our Methodist teenage interviewees told us of two of her friends who had left: 'really they just don't feel the church has anything relevant to them.' It would be wrong, however, to conclude that people will be satisfied with oversimplistic answers to the issues that concern them. Josephine Mason found that her charismatic Anglican church's attitude to life's problems was 'unreal' and lacking in pragmatism. The answer to every problem seemed to be: ' "prayer will solve it, just keep smiling through", [whilst] what you actually wanted to hear somebody say was, "I've had a real bitch of a day today, and I've really got to talk these problems through, and I know it would actually help me feel better if I pray a bit, but I know, on the other hand, that I have to sort my own problems out!" ' If a church's teachings, however impressive they may be, fail to enable people to engage their faith with their everyday life, with its hopes and fears, successes and failures, the church itself may eventually be discarded as 'irrelevant'.

### Listening to the statistics

Our questionnaire respondents were asked to look at a battery of 198 statements and to identify those which best described why there had been a dropping off in their church going. The questionnaire asked a set of eighty-seven questions specifically designed to survey aspects of *unfulfilled expectations of the church*. From this set we have chosen forty-two typical questions, reflecting the general spread of responses. The forty-two questions are discussed within seven groups, concerned with blame attached to the church (table 9.1), worship expectations (table 9.2), pastoral care expectations (table 9.3), leadership style expectations (table 9.4), teaching expectations (table 9.5), lack of relevance (table 9.6) and openness to change (table 9.7). In these tables we separate the respondents into two categories, depending on whether they left before the age of twenty or later in life. The figures in each column are percentages of that category.

The statistics in table 9.1 show that a much higher proportion of church leavers absolve the church from responsibility for their leaving than wish to blame the church. Thus, around one in ten of those who left before the age of twenty and one in five of those who left later in life attribute their leaving to the church having failed them in some way. By way of contrast over three-fifths of all respondents affirm that it was not the church's fault that they dropped off.

Table 9.1:  Blame attached to the church

|  | Under 20 % | 20 and over % |
|---|---|---|
| The church had failed me in some way | 11 | 20 |
| I changed – it wasn't the church's fault that I dropped off | 66 | 60 |

The statistics in table 9.2 show that unfulfilled expectations relating to worship are a more significant cause for church leaving before the age of twenty than later in life. Among those who had left church before the age of twenty, between two-fifths and one-half had felt that the worship was too mechanical, while a third had felt the worship was too formal. By way of contrast, among those who left church later in life, almost as many did so complaining that the worship was too informal as did so complaining that the worship was too formal. One in four of all respondents attribute their church leaving to the experience that there was too little sense of the presence of God in worship.

Table 9.2:   Worship expectations

|  | Under 20 % | 20 and over % |
|---|---|---|
| I disliked the church's style of worship | 30 | 20 |
| I felt the worship was too mechanical | 44 | 26 |
| I felt that there was too little sense of the presence of God in worship | 28 | 25 |
| I felt that there was not enough variety in worship to suit different tastes | 22 | 20 |
| I felt that the worship was too formal | 34 | 20 |
| I felt that the worship was too informal | 4 | 13 |

The statistics in table 9.3 show that unfulfilled expectations relating to pastoral care are a more significant cause for church leaving in adult life than before the age of twenty. One in four of those leaving church later in life had failed to find the church caring and supportive. One in five of those leaving church later in life had felt let down by the church at a time when they needed its support. One in six of those leaving church later in life felt that the clergy did not provide sufficient care for them. One in sixteen of all respondents had found the church's pastoral care of them to be unprofessional.

The statistics in table 9.4 show that unfulfilled expectations relating to leadership style play a stronger role in church leaving before the age of twenty than later in life. One in four of those leaving before the age of twenty had found the style of the church to be too authoritarian. One in three of those leaving before the age of twenty had found the church to be too hierarchical and status-conscious. About a quarter of all respondents had been influenced in their decision to leave by the view that the church did not allow women their rightful place in decision making.

Table 9.3:   Pastoral care expectations

|  | Under 20 % | 20 and over % |
|---|---|---|
| I felt let down by the church at a time when I needed its support | 12 | 19 |
| I did not find the church to be caring and supportive | 22 | 25 |
| The clergy did not provide sufficient care for me | 12 | 17 |
| I felt misdirected by the church when I needed its support | 10 | 15 |
| The church's pastoral care to me was unprofessional | 6 | 7 |
| The church's pastoral care to others was unprofessional | 7 | 6 |

Table 9.4:   Leadership style expectations

|  | Under 20 % | 20 and over % |
|---|---|---|
| The leadership style of the church was too authoritarian | 27 | 20 |
| The church did not take enough account of church tradition | 4 | 12 |
| The church did not take enough account of the will of God | 5 | 12 |
| The church was too hierarchical and status-conscious | 32 | 26 |
| The church did not allow women their rightful place in decision-making | 31 | 21 |
| The church leadership was not giving a clear enough sense of direction | 18 | 15 |

The statistics in table 9.5 show that unfulfilled expectations relating to the church's teaching were generally more likely to be reported by those who had left before the age of twenty than by those who left later in life. A third of those who left before the age of twenty had disagreed with the church's theological teaching, while half of them had disagreed with the church's stance on key moral issues. Two-fifths of those who had left under the age of twenty had found the church too conservative. Among those who left later in life, one in four had found the church too conservative and one in ten had found the church too liberal. One in ten of all respondents complained that the church did not seem to take sin seriously enough.

**Table 9.5:  Teaching expectations**

|  | Under 20 % | 20 and over % |
|---|---|---|
| I disagreed with the church's theological teachings | 34 | 19 |
| I disagreed with the church's stance on key moral issues | 47 | 33 |
| The church was too liberal for me | 3 | 10 |
| The church was too conservative for me | 39 | 27 |
| The church did not seem to take sin seriously enough | 10 | 11 |
| The church's moral teachings were too narrow | 38 | 26 |

The statistics in table 9.6 show that the relevance of the church was more likely to have been questioned by those who had left before the age of twenty than by those who had left later in life. Three-fifths of those who left before the age of twenty say that the church failed to connect with the rest of their life or that they were bored with the church. Half of them had found the church's teaching and sermons irrelevant to their everyday life. Among those who left later in life, two-fifths had felt that the church failed to connect with the rest of their life.

The statistics in table 9.7 show that change in the church was more likely to be resented by those who left later in life than by those who left before the age of twenty. Around a quarter of those who left later in life had disliked new hymns, new service books or new translations of the Bible. By way of contrast, those who left before the age of twenty were more likely to complain that the church was too reluctant to change. Around two-fifths of those

**Table 9.6:  Lack of relevance**

|  | Under 20 % | 20 and over % |
|---|---|---|
| The church failed to connect with the rest of my life | 62 | 40 |
| Sermons were irrelevant to my everyday life | 52 | 35 |
| The church's teaching was irrelevant to my everyday life | 49 | 28 |
| I was bored | 58 | 29 |
| Church felt like 'another planet' | 36 | 16 |
| I was not interested in the activities on offer | 50 | 41 |

**Table 9.7:  Openness to change**

|  | Under 20 % | 20 and over % |
|---|---|---|
| I did not like the direction in which the church was going | 25 | 26 |
| I did not like changes that had happened in the church | 15 | 28 |
| I did not like the new hymns | 17 | 26 |
| I did not like the new service book | 13 | 24 |
| I did not like the new translation of the Bible | 15 | 25 |
| I did not like the new style of worship | 11 | 21 |
| The church was too old-fashioned | 40 | 19 |
| The church was stuck in its views | 45 | 30 |
| The church did not allow people to discuss or disagree with its views | 34 | 25 |
| I felt powerless to bring about change within the church | 29 | 24 |

who left before the age of twenty had felt that the church was too old-fashioned and stuck in its views. Over a quarter of all respondents reported that the church had not allowed people to discuss or disagree with its views.

## Summary

In this chapter we have seen that disillusionment can result when expectations of the church are not fulfilled. Sometimes the expectations are impossible or unrealistically high. Sometimes the church is expected to meet all kinds of extrinsic needs, minimally related to its primary function. But, equally, sometimes it fails to meet legitimate needs. Church leavers will often complain, sometimes very vehemently, at their church's pastoral neglect or abuse, its lack of relevance, its style of worship, its leadership style, its teachings, its hypocrisy and its unwillingness to change. In some cases, one suspects, this simply represents self-justification after the event, but the theme is too widespread and too strong to ignore – some church leaving, at least, results from disillusionment with a church that fails to be authentic and does not manage to live up to its ideals. Other church leavers, however, make it quite clear that it is *not* the church that is at fault in their case. A multi-dimensional approach to church leaving cannot be avoided.

# 10   Believing but not Belonging

One important way in which churches sustain commitment among their members is to offer them a sense of belonging. In a society of high geographical mobility and rapid change, the church can be a much-needed source of close friendships and supportive networks, especially for the isolated nuclear family and those on their own. The church can even, as it were, take the place of a person's far-away family, offering support in times of crisis and a regular 'family' atmosphere. Human beings have an abiding need to feel that they belong somewhere. When churches fail to offer them this sense of belonging, people often prefer to leave.

Church leaving is frequently related to the perception that relationships within the church are no longer close and supportive – indeed they may be disturbingly conflictual. Several studies have demonstrated the importance of this factor for church leaving. John Savage (1976:68) concluded that dropping out is usually triggered by conflict with the clergy, another family member, or another church member. Warren J. Hartman (1976:40) discovered that the most frequently given reason by those who had dropped out of church was 'their failure to feel that they were accepted, loved or wanted. They felt that they did not belong and that others in the church and church school did not demonstrate any real love and concern for them.' This was particularly apparent among people under thirty years old. There is reason, however, to be somewhat wary of generalising these findings. Both the studies cited, by Savage and Hartman, were of United Methodist Church leavers in the United States. As Dean R. Hoge (1981:12) has noted in his own study of Catholic dropouts: 'relationships with other parishioners were more important in these studies than they are for typical Catholics.' There has always been a strong emphasis within the Methodist Church on achieving a 'warm, supportive Christian community' (Hartman 1976:42). As a popular Methodist hymn expresses it: 'All praise to our redeeming Lord, who joins us by his grace.'

Some would argue that the provision of a sense of belonging is not the primary function of a church. The Church exists first and foremost to witness to the Word made flesh and to enable people to find salvation and ultimate meaning for their existence. Most churches also offer people a sense of belonging, but this is a secondary function which they perform. Some churches take pride in describing themselves as a 'church family' or 'fellowship' or 'Christian community'. Each of these terms wrestles to express in English the meaning of the New Testament word *koinonia*, the term used by the earliest Christians to describe the quality of relationship Christians were to have in their common life together. St Paul summarised this in Philippians: 'complete my joy by being of the same mind, having the same love, being in full accord' (Philippians 2:2). The Roman Catholic Church has emphasised the communal dimension of the Church as the *People of God*, especially since the Second Vatican Council. Were a church to neglect completely its responsibility to foster *koinonia* one would begin to doubt if it was properly performing its primary function, but, nonetheless, some would maintain that the creation of community and the provision of a sense of belonging are secondary functions.

It is true that belonging often precedes believing for new recruits. Formal admission to membership or full communion of a church does, however, generally involve assent to what the church is primarily about. At the point of entry into the church a person would be unlikely, at least publicly, to cite the need for a sense of belonging as his or her primary motive for joining. Interestingly, as Carl Dudley (1979:78) has remarked, there is therefore a curious double standard operating: 'When people unite with a congregation . . . they consciously relate church membership with programme participation and religious values. When they leave, however, they are more likely to blame a breakdown in personal relationships.'

## Losing the sense of belonging

In this chapter we shall be focusing on those who have not necessarily lost their beliefs, but have lost the sense of belonging. People join churches, at least partly, for social reasons. Some leave when their expectations of finding friendship and community are dashed or remain unfulfilled. As Carl Dudley concluded in his study, *Where Have All Our People Gone?*, unless church members receive what he terms the 'three strokes' – recognition, esteem and a sense of belonging – they may feel let down and will drop out (Dudley 1979:78).

Most of the clergy whom we interviewed recognised the importance of such factors. John Ingram, a vicar on a housing estate, told us that his aim was to 'create an environment where people feel comfortable'. He stressed the importance of building relationships: 'The main reason that people leave church is that they don't make friends and relationships within the congregation, then it's very easy for those people to drift out.' Unfortunately the church is not always successful in creating a warm, supportive community.

Sarah Johnson, a married woman in her early thirties, left her Anglican church whilst complaining of a sense of isolation: 'When the children were born there was only one of the children's godparents from the church who bothered to visit, and at the time I was feeling very low.' It was when her mother died, who had been very active in the church, that she felt particularly let down: 'When she died my world fell apart, but I thought at least I'll get the support of the church, the church will be there for me, the church will uphold my family through this. [But] we didn't get the support, we didn't get help that we needed, and that came like a double blow at that time. And that's when we came to the realisation that this really isn't right. We've not got the relationship here that we ought to have with other Christians.' Sarah switched to a New Church where she felt 'really welcomed' and where she has found 'true friends that I know I could turn to anytime, night or day'.

Justine Sullivan left the Anglican Church for a New Religious Movement because she was impressed by the quality of relationships there: 'They were really nice and very friendly and down to earth. I thought this was wonderful, to meet such nice people. There must be something good about it . . . it must be true.' One of our interviewees, Kate White, was actually asked to leave by her Baptist church. Not surprisingly, this enforced exclusion caused her to question her church going: 'I came to the conclusion that there wasn't an awful lot in going to church!'

Sometimes people do not feel they properly belong if the membership of a church is socially, racially, sexually or age-imbalanced, in a way that makes them feel marginalised or obtrusive. Although churches, in theory, welcome people of every background and the gospel is to do with overcoming human barriers, there tend, for good sociological reasons, to be geographical and denominational differences in the social class composition of congregations. A Methodist church in the inner city will have a rather different social class make-up than one in the stockbroker belt. Anglican churches will generally attract people of a higher social class than Methodist churches – an under-recognised component of continuing ecumenical divisions! 'I disliked the fact that a certain amount of class distinction existed, and that most of the officers of the church use it as part of their social climb', one male leaver in his mid-fifties told a Methodist survey in the 1960s (Butler 1966:239).

Black immigrants have sometimes found British churches unwelcoming and even hostile. 'There is no visible involvement of blacks ... in [church] leadership ... Racism ... will continue to fertilise the decline in growth of the Church unless audacious and radical steps are taken', complained one correspondent to the *Methodist Recorder*.[1] Although, as St Paul proclaimed, in the Christian community 'there is neither male nor female' (Galatians 3:28), women have felt alienated from male-dominated churches and men have felt out of place in churches where the majority of worshippers are women, and, one might add, elderly. In many churches there are few people in their twenties or their thirties or their forties. 'Congregations are pitiful and full of old people, and new young families want nothing to do with them' a 1993 study concluded.[2]

The teenagers whom we interviewed told us that one reason friends had stopped going to church was because 'there are old people there [and] they don't like old people'. There were not enough people of *their* age. Wayne, a Methodist teenager from the south-east, told us: 'It seems to be the older people who go to church, and, if they keep the attitude they've got now towards it, then it'll gradually go down hill, and die.' Young people often expressed disappointment that church worship felt culturally alien and 'old fashioned'. Many preferred 'more lively', 'exciting', 'creative', 'youth-orientated', 'alternative' services and complained that 'church services are boring, especially for people our age'. Another Methodist teenager, Dave, told us 'there were quite a few people my age ... but then our services, like for our age, got stopped, and they just didn't come along any more'. 'It was just all boring. The minister was like really old and miserable,' complained one youngster.

Older people also felt excluded, sometimes by the very things that made young people feel at home. Matthew Williams, a New Church leaver, felt he had outgrown singing choruses and, finding himself in a congregation where 'the majority of people [were] a lot younger' and where there were a lot of students he decided: 'I just couldn't handle all these young happy people. I just thought, "I can't stick this", so I left and that was the last time I went to church.'

For Sarah Johnson it was the 'big age gap' between her and the others in the church that mattered: 'There wasn't anyone our age. The next married couple to us were in their forties, but they were old forties . . . The next youngest under us is actually our babysitter now, who is just eighteen.' Although churches often refer to themselves as a 'family' they do not always resemble a normal, all-age multi-generational family. In any case, the 'family' metaphor for the church must be treated with care, for it can appear to 'exclude the contribution of single people' (General Synod Board of Mission 1996:24).

One has only to read the letters of St Paul to recognise that the church always has a tendency to break into factions and to form cliques (for instance, 1 Corinthians 1:10–16). Sometimes these factions will exercise considerable power in the church. It may be more important for someone to belong to this 'in group' and to enjoy their respect than to belong to the church *per se*. Where people feel excluded from such groups this may be an important motive for their leaving the church. Josephine and Charles Mason told us of their experience in a charismatic Anglican church. They had joined, and initially enjoyed, an *Alpha* course, but couldn't attend the residential weekend that was part of the course. 'When the group reconvened the following week, it was a bit like being strangers at a party really because everybody had moved on in this huge way, they'd all bonded together spiritually . . . And I think that was the beginning of the end . . . People we had got to know in our group and the leaders would be superficially polite, but they weren't really terribly interested in us, because we obviously weren't part of their particular club any longer.' Josephine told us: 'I left because I didn't have the right credentials, I didn't belong.'

Sometimes leavers report that they did not feel properly valued

by the church. They complain that their opinions were not listened
to. It was always other people who were asked to sit on committees
or to take on leadership functions, and they themselves had never
been approached. A Methodist study in the mid 1960s found that
those who had never been given 'positions of responsibility and
leadership' were most likely to lapse (Butler 1966:242–3).[3] Young
people told us that the church 'wasn't really open' to them. One
told us: 'I think we should be involved more, and asked what we
feel and what we think.' Methodist young people, still within the
church, told us they appreciated the opportunity offered by *Charter*
*'95* to be involved, with people of all ages, in developing a shared
vision for their church.

Equally, some leavers have held positions of leadership in their
church, which they have, willingly or unwillingly, relinquished.
They may find it difficult to come to terms with the loss of status
involved or resent the lack of appreciation shown by the church
for their past labours. Martyn Evans, a vicar in suburban London,
spoke of the 'swathe of really quite well established older middle-
aged people' in his church who had left 'because their role had
either vanished, because we don't need them to do that any more,
or else it's been taken over by younger people who have come in
more recently, and who appear to them to be perhaps more
welcome than they are now'. 'I think there are some people who
feel that if they can't actually run the church, then they don't want
to be part of it at all!' he reflected.

Conflict with church leaders sometimes underlies a person's
leaving. In some cases it is simply a matter of a personality clash
with the vicar. In other cases the leadership behaves in a way likely
to undermine a person's sense of belonging. The leaver may have
been personally humiliated by one of the church leaders, even, in
the case of one of our interviewees, physically attacked. Bullying
is not confined to the school playground. It can take place in
workplaces and churches too. In the case of Nicholas White, his
New Church minister made it painfully clear to him that he and
his wife were unsuitable to run a youth group. When Nicholas
questioned what he saw as the minister's extremely undemocratic
and devious leadership style, he was excommunicated or, in the
church's terms, 'dis-fellowshipped'. 'It was just unbelievable. He'd
preached against me from the pulpit, and it culminated in his wife
slapping me round the face in public, just because I was arguing
with her husband.' Ironically, Nicholas had first been attracted to

the Christian faith when he was nineteen, because of 'the way [Christians] cared about one another and loved one another'.

There are at least four areas of perceived imbalance within churches that can motivate someone to leave. These are imbalances between: (1) involvement and passivity; (2) intimacy and anonymity; (3) plant and congregation size; and (4) inclusiveness and exclusiveness. Individuals are prone to leave when they perceive the church to be tipping the balance too far in what they see as the wrong direction. We shall examine each of these in turn.

## Involvement and passivity

For some people their sense of belonging may derive from intense involvement in the life of their church. They may, for instance, hold a leadership position in the church; or their life may revolve around attending church services and activities; or their church's worship style may evoke especially active physical, intellectual and/or spiritual participation. For other people their sense of belonging may be nourished by a more passive role and they may, for instance, prefer to spectate, rather than to participate actively, in worship. This does not necessarily diminish their sense of belonging to a wider Christian community, much as the concert goer at a performance of Handel's *Messiah* may become aware that they are part of an attentive audience, both within the concert hall and also of all those, whether still on earth or now in heaven, who have ever enjoyed the oratorio. Each individual will want the balance between involvement and passivity to be set slightly differently. It is when the church's balance tips too far in the 'wrong' direction that a person may choose to leave. Worship for instance may become too passive or too participatory. Change in either direction will risk alienating some individuals.

The young people whom we interviewed often wanted to take a more active role in their churches. Worship was experienced as too passive. Some young people would only return to church if there was more 'involvement . . . maybe taking some services, or not just being talked down to like you're a child' and if young people were 'made to feel that [they] have an important role in the church'. Wesley Harris, an ex-Methodist, who first came to England as a child, missed the participatory style of worship to which he had been accustomed in Africa. Worship in Britain was 'more of a sombre, sober, serious effort', controlled by the minister. He complained that the congregation just 'sit there, listen . . . sing, sit down [and] listen some more'.

Conversely, some leavers had felt too involved. Deborah Clarke, an ex-Anglican lay-reader, told us that she was living 'with the tension of how do you live most deeply in community and . . . most deeply in yourself?' and admitted, 'Maybe I'm swinging too hard onto one side at the moment' after her withdrawal from church involvement. Gareth Wilkinson, a stressed businessman and ex-Methodist, found his church's expectation of intense involvement to be intrusive: 'I wish to be able to go to church without it having to become my life . . . What I find is you can't just go to church and be an individual. You can't just go along and exercise your wish to take part in the worship. People always want to know who you are.' He described his visit to a Methodist church where 'I was, I can only say, I suppose the polite term is "canvassed", and I've no doubt the people that pursued me thought they were making me welcome, or perhaps they were trying to recruit me, but it was really quite intrusive . . . they were not content to accept the fact that I might just want to go to church on an occasional basis, but not get any further involvement.'

## Intimacy and anonymity

Some people will be more at home in the intimacy of an intensely expressive church fellowship, where people are, as it were, expected to wear their spiritual hearts on their sleeves. Others will feel more comfortable in the relatively anonymous setting of a cathedral, where there are plenty of 'pillars' to hide behind. One can attend a cathedral service without speaking to another soul, without signing a visitors' book, and even without standing up and singing hymns. The cathedral goer would probably be horrified at what he or she would regard as the claustrophobic nature of the intimacy of the church fellowship, whilst, conversely, the fellowship goer would regard the anonymity of cathedral worship as horrifyingly impersonal. There is the danger that church fellowships can become too personally intrusive and their leadership over-parental. Heavy-handed 'shepherding' within some New Churches has alienated some. Equally, cathedral worship can become so privatised that it loses touch with the social dimension of the gospel. A sense of belonging may be linked partly to the physical size of the church building and the size of the congregation worshipping there – over-large churches can be too impersonal, over-small churches can be claustrophobic. Individuals will be prone to leave if the particular balance between intimacy and anonymity to which they have become accustomed is disturbed, or if they move and cannot find a church with their preferred balance.

Elsie Brooks, a Methodist minister, told us of the two churches of which she had oversight. One was a large town-centre church with a membership of over two hundred. The other was in a 'village' location and had less than one hundred members. The first church alienated some people because they perceived it as 'too big and impersonal'. The 'family atmosphere' of the second church alienated others because it was 'a bit too close and claustrophobic' and didn't appear to offer them 'freedom to be themselves'. Sarah Johnson described her experience of visiting both types of church. After moving house Sarah and her husband tried out a 'huge church' which was 'also very unfriendly, in the fact that you had to watch which pew you sat in, in case that was Mrs Y's or whoever's'. Later she went to a New Church and found the welcome more personal, but stifling: 'We were welcomed with open arms, but welcomed too much, in the fact that ... in the service we were actually welcomed by name, and made to stand up, and it was, "Hi, Sarah and the children are here today and the husband Trevor's not with them because he's had to go to work today, but hopefully we'll see him next week?" It was like, "Oh, my goodness, I can't cope with this, I need the ground to open up and swallow me." I think it was too much the other way.'

Some churches may be working with an outdated notion of themselves as a kind of surrogate 'village community'. This may be attractive to some, but others will fail to connect with this, given that people's lives today are lived, not so much in community, but in separate, and sometimes overlapping, 'networks' – work, home, leisure, family, education, religion maybe. There is also the 'virtual' connectedness of the Internet. Life is no longer a matter of close face-to-face personal relationships. The church may need to take into account those who 'desire a distant, formal and self-protecting way of relating' (General Synod Board of Mission 1996:28), as well as those who yearn for lost community.

## Plant and congregation size

A factor in church leaving only recently recognised by sociologists is the potential imbalance between the seating capacity of a church and the number of worshippers in the congregation. All too often the size of church congregations is pitifully small, compared with the size of the church building. The church itself often dates from the last century and was probably ambitiously large even when it was first built. The American humorist, Garrison Keillor, once memorably described such a church as 'fifteen worshippers in the pews, scattered, like a connect-the-dots picture' (Keillor 1994:251). Not surprisingly, where congregations are small and church buildings large, people can soon feel a sense of coldness and impersonality. It is easy to conclude that the church is a 'dying cause' and the evident sparsity of people tends to underline the fact that church going is unfashionable.

Robin Gill (1993), in his book *The Myth of the Empty Church*, has called into question previous assumptions, or 'myths' as he terms them, about the origin of (nearly) empty churches. It is tempting, but much too simplistic, to attribute empty churches to the general decline in church going in an increasingly secular society. In fact, his extensive historical analysis of both church going statistics and seating capacities has led Gill to argue that empty churches are not so much an *effect* of church going decline as one of the *causes*. Even before the First World War most churches were 'more empty than full'. The 'competitive church building between denominations'[4] of the Victorian era over-provided in urban as well as rural areas. Free Church chapels were already too large for their congregations, even before the church going rate began to decline. As Gill (1992:105) points out: 'Too many churches inevitably means emptier churches [and] empty churches themselves may act as agents of overall decline in church-going.'

Empty churches act as agents of overall decline in at least two ways. First, empty or redundant churches tend to reinforce public perceptions that religion is a thing of the past. Secondly, sparsely attended churches, often with overwhelmingly elderly and female congregations, may prove daunting to marginal church goers. As one of our young interviewees put it: '[Mine is] a really small village church and there's about ten people in the congregation who are all over seventy, and it's just you don't really want to go to an atmosphere like that.' The legacy of over-provision of large Victorian churches is evidently a mixed blessing!

## Inclusiveness and exclusiveness

Some people prefer to belong to an inclusive church, with fluid boundaries and few doctrinal hurdles for members to negotiate. Other people prefer the lines between church and world, and between believer and non-believer, to be more rigidly drawn. Many Anglican churches would think of themselves as part of a 'broad Church', the very attraction of which is that 'because so little is ruled out, so much can be ruled in'.[5] There are, however, other less inclusive wings of the Anglican Communion – biblical fundamentalists, charismatic evangelicals, liberal evangelicals, liberal catholics and traditional catholics – and the trend towards 'gathered' Anglican churches, based on a particular tradition or style of worship, risks 'disenfranchising the nominal' (General Synod Board of Mission 1996:32). However inclusive the Christian gospel is in theory, in practice it has often become sectarian and indeed the very cohesion of Christian communities has sometimes been secured by rejection or demonisation of others. The inter-religious conflict in Northern Ireland is a sad reflection of this. People's sense of belonging to their church is sometimes associated with a strong 'us versus them' divide. For others it is the radically inclusive nature of their church that is so appealing. Any change in the current balance between inclusiveness and exclusiveness may cause either party to reconsider their church involvement.

Richard Elliott, an Anglican leaver, explained to us that he had left because of the lack of clear moral boundaries in the Church's teaching and practice. He cited the example of a vicar with a 'live-in [male] lover': 'If the Church won't point out that God regards these activities as sinful, nobody else is, and they're falling down . . . by just going along with the world.' By contrast, others we interviewed complained that the Church was not inclusive enough. Arron Coates, a young Catholic leaver, was particularly concerned about his Church's treatment of women: 'I really don't want to be part of the Church where most of the women don't have an active role to play . . . unless they're prepared to play second-fiddle to men.' He also felt very strongly about the effective exclusion of his grandmother from the church after her divorce:

'My nan never set foot in church again after being divorced, because she felt it was a shameful state to be in [and] that the Church looked down upon her. Apart from going at Christmas, she didn't go back in until she died. She'd come from a very Catholic background... was a brilliant Catholic, Christian person... [Before] she used to go to church every night of the week.' Deborah Clarke had first left church after listening to the final sermon at her boarding school, which outraged her. The message was: 'if you choose your friends unwisely, you will be rejected by your friends and family.' This was a church that threatened exclusion, rather than the inclusion she instinctively associated with the gospel.

## Attractive alternatives

We have been looking at ways in which church leaving can be a response to the failure of the church to provide, at least in the leaver's estimation, a proper sense of belonging. Sometimes, however, leaving may be less a reflection on the quality of relationships within the church and more to do with the attraction of other providers of a sense of belonging. Sometimes the leaver finds it more important to belong to another group than to the church. Young people, for instance, may prefer to identify with their peer group. They may perceive the church as associated with a previous generation and attach much more importance to how their friends think and behave. What counts is to be accepted by their peers. Their worst fear is to be ostracised or to be thought odd by their friends or their fellow students at school or college. It is more important, for instance, to be fashionable than to be warm. Given that church going is not particularly fashionable in Britain there is always the danger that young people will be teased or bullied if it is known that they go to church. As ex-Methodist Wesley Harris put it, church goers tend to get 'grouped with the anoraks!' Not surprisingly, many young people prefer to belong to their peer group, rather than to the church. The two are of course, in theory, not incompatible, but in practice many young people choose to avoid the potential conflict. Older people may find their need for a sense of belonging is better met by the badminton club, the bridge set or the golf club and decide that there is nothing else to keep them in the church.

Our teenage interviewees often told us about the peer pressure they experienced. Church going was 'not trendy' and people tended to be teased about it. As Jason told us: 'Some of my friends used to go [to church], but, now we've gone to high school, if they get teased they don't go to church.' Peer pressure appears to decline as people get older. As Tom, a young Methodist, told us: 'My friends know where I go on a Sunday morning. But, as I'm in the sixth form now, it's more understood, because people are left to do what they want in the sixth form, so there's not much peer pressure.' What matters, especially to younger teenagers, is what their friends are doing. As Emma pointed out, this can work both ways: 'People might start going back to church if they get in with friends who are going to church – they might be encouraged to give it another try.'

It is not only young people who find it hard to go to church if their friends do not attend. As Dorothy King, an elderly widow, told us, during her married life she had not gone to church, because 'nobody I knew went to church and I wouldn't go on my own'. Recently, after she had moved to a retirement flat that happened to be situated next to a church, she had been invited to the 'Ladies Fellowship' and had begun to get to know people in the church. She now felt able to attend church, after a lifetime's absence, without feeling 'self-conscious'. Church going that is dependent on the presence of a person's friends is, nevertheless, inevitably vulnerable if those friends move away or die.

## Listening to the statistics

Our questionnaire respondents were asked to look at a battery of 198 statements and to identify those which best described why there had been a dropping off in their church going. The questionnaire asked a set of twenty-four questions specifically designed to survey *belonging factors*. From this set we have chosen eight typical questions, reflecting the general spread of responses. In table 10 we separate the respondents into two categories, depending on whether they left before the age of twenty or later in life. The figures in each column are percentages of that category.

The statistics demonstrate that factors concerned with belonging operate somewhat differently among the two age groups. Belonging factors more likely to be cited as reasons for leaving

**Table 10:  Belonging**

|  | Under20 % | 20 and over % |
|---|---|---|
| I did not feel a part of the church | 58 | 47 |
| There were cliques or 'in groups' from which I felt excluded | 16 | 26 |
| There were not enough people of my age | 16 | 13 |
| The church did not listen to me | 16 | 13 |
| Most of my friends were not church goers | 48 | 40 |
| I felt church going was unfashionable | 19 | 3 |
| The church was too negative towards the 'world outside' | 31 | 21 |
| I felt there should be a clearer line drawn between Christian values and the values of the 'outside world' | 23 | 26 |

church under the age of twenty include not feeling part of the church, finding that most of their friends were not church goers, and recognising church going to be unfashionable. On the other hand, the feeling that there were cliques or 'in groups' from which they felt excluded was more likely to be cited as a reason for leaving church later in life than before the age of twenty. The view that the church was too negative towards the 'world outside' was more likely to be cited as a reason for leaving before the age of twenty than later in life. On the other hand, the view that the church was failing to draw a clear enough line between Christian values and the values of the 'outside world' was more likely to be cited as a reason for leaving later in life than before the age of twenty. Between two-fifths and half of all respondents cite as a reason for leaving church the fact that most of their friends were not church goers. An even higher proportion, half of all respondents, cite as a reason for leaving church the fact that they did not feel part of the church.

## Summary

In this chapter we have explored the importance of a sense of belonging for many who attend church. Where the church fails to satisfy this hunger, or where other groups or organisations appear to be better at offering a sense of belonging, this can be a reason to drop out of church attendance. As we have seen, a 'sense of belonging' means different things to different people. It is no easy task to get the balance right!

# 11 Leaving and Returning

In the preceding chapters we have made good use of the information provided by the respondents to our questionnaire. In this questionnaire, church leavers assessed the importance of 198 factors which may have been associated with their reason for leaving church. Two further important clues may be discovered concerning church leaving and church returning from closer inspection of the replies to these questions.

The present chapter, therefore, proposes to return to these questionnaires with two specific questions in mind. First, is it possible to identify the main precipitating reasons behind church leaving and to distinguish these main precipitating reasons from the host of other associated factors? Second, is it possible to detect a relationship between the causes cited for leaving church and an individual church leaver's likelihood of returning?

## Main precipitating reasons

As we have seen, in chapters three to ten, when people are asked why they have left church, they cite a variety of different reasons. Some of these reasons may not be the key reason for their church leaving. They may be predisposing, but not precipitating, factors. In order to try to gauge the main precipitating factors we also invited questionnaire respondents to specify 'just one main reason' for their leaving by identifying which of the 198 statements summed up this reason most clearly.

In order to make sense of our questionnaire respondents' answers to this particular exercise, we grouped the individual statements into the eight major clusters of reasons identified in chapters three to ten. All told, 193 of the 198 items were intended to fall into these eight clusters.

The statistics in table 11 summarise what we found by undertaking this particular analysis. Three pieces of information are provided in this table. In the first column we identify the number of items within the questionnaire's battery of 198 statements which relate to the given cluster. For example, there were thirteen items in the questionnaire concerned with loss of faith as a cause for church leaving. In the second column we identify the percentage of our respondents leaving at any age who specified one of the reasons within the given cluster as their main reason for leaving. For example, 18 per cent of the total group of church leavers identified loss of faith as the main reason for leaving the church. The figures in this column do not add up to 100 per cent because around one in five of the respondents to the questionnaire did not feel able to cite just one main reason for their leaving. In the third column we identify the percentage of our respondents leaving at the age of twenty or over who specified one of the reasons in the given cluster as their main reason for leaving. For example, 16 per cent of those leaving at the age of twenty or over identified loss of faith as their main reason for leaving.

**Table 11:  The precipitating reasons for leaving**

| Cluster | Questionnaire items | Leaving at any age % | Leaving after age of 20 % |
|---|---|---|---|
| Loss of faith | 13 | 18 | 16 |
| Changing values | 23 | 9 | 9 |
| Stage of faith | 10 | 6 | 1 |
| Changes and chances | 19 | 21 | 22 |
| Childhood upbringing | 1 | 1 | 1 |
| High cost | 16 | 1 | 1 |
| Unfulfilled expectations | 87 | 22 | 26 |
| Belonging factors | 24 | 2 | 1 |

The statistics in table 11 show that respondents' expressed main reasons are not distributed evenly between our clusters. The precipitating reason is most likely to be connected with *unfulfilled expectations*, or *changes and chances*, or *loss of faith*. These findings offer churches an important insight into the priorities which may be most effective in pastoral strategy to address the problem of church leaving.

### Church returning

While just over half (55 per cent) of the respondents to our questionnaire who had left churches were clear that they would not be
returning, the other 45 per cent were leaving the possibility of
returning open. Our analysis of their replies demonstrates that the
likelihood of returning to church is closely related to the original
reason for leaving. In other words, individuals who have left for
certain reasons are more likely to return than individuals who have
left for other reasons.

Put most simply, the data suggest that knowing why people
have left church allows us to identify three main categories of
church leavers: those *most* likely to consider returning, those *least*
likely to consider returning, and those who display *average* likelihood of returning.

## *Most likelihood of returning*

Church leavers who are *most* likely to return are those who have
left for reasons we have described as changes and chances. Typically these are individuals who moved to a new area and either
got out of the habit of church going or failed to find a church in
the new area which they liked. Other individuals in this category
have stopped going to church because of increasing pressure from
work or family. Some say that their work schedule interfered with
attendance at church, that their partner was not attending church,
or that their children needed them to provide transport on
Sundays.

Four other categories of church leavers are also more likely than
average to consider returning to church. One category are those
who left because they felt that there were not enough people of
their own age in the congregation. The second category are those
who left because they had become involved in taking illegal drugs.
The third category are those who felt pressured to leave because
the church was making increasing demands on their money. The
fourth category are those who felt that the church was failing to
cater properly for their children's needs.

### Least likelihood of returning

Church leavers who are *least* likely to return have left church for one of six main reasons. The first main reason concerns the quest for personal authenticity. These are the people who say that they could not keep going to church and be true to themselves, or that they felt their own values were no longer compatible with participation in the church.

The second main reason concerns the loss of faith. These are the people who say quite directly that they doubted, questioned or lost their faith, questioned the church's doctrinal or moral teachings; others found the church's teaching difficult to reconcile with modern science or with the truth claims of other world faiths.

The third main reason concerned the relegation of church to the domain of childhood. These are the people who say that they were made to go to church by their parents and it put them off, or that they grew up and started making decisions on their own.

The fourth main reason identified those individuals who had never been deeply committed to the church in the first place. These are the people who say that their main motivations for going to church were not religious.

The fifth main reason concerns radical disenchantment with the church. These are the people who say that they were disillusioned by the church's failure to live up to its ideals, by the church's materialism, by the church's abuse of power and wealth, or by the church's attitude towards women, homosexuality or racism.

The sixth main reason identified those who had grown to see the church as fundamentally irrelevant to life. These are the people who say that the church's teaching, worship and preaching failed to connect with the rest of their life. For them the church felt like 'another planet'.

### Average likelihood of returning

Midway between those church leavers most likely and least likely to return are those who display *average* likelihood of returning. Individuals in this category have left church for one of seven main reasons.

The first group left church because they felt marginalised by their church. These are the people who say that the church did not value what they had to offer, or that the church did not listen to them, or that they were not allowed to play an active part in the church.

The second group left church because they felt let down by God. These are the people who say that they could not reconcile their own suffering with their belief in God, or that God had let them down in some other way.

The third group left church because they felt that their lifestyle was not compatible with participation in the church. These are the people who say that their marriage broke down, that they were having sex outside marriage, or that they were in a sexually active same-sex relationship.

The fourth group left church because they felt that the church was out of step with their own stage of faith development. These are the people who say that the church was no longer helping them to grow, or that they felt spiritually out of their depth in their church. For some the church's teaching may have been too simplified and unchallenging; while for others the church's teaching may have failed to give them the certainty they were seeking.

The fifth group left church because they felt burned out by their leadership role and responsibilities. These are the people who say that they felt emotionally drained by their leadership role or that they were finding it increasingly difficult to listen to others and to care for them.

The sixth group left church because they had grown dissatisfied with the local church's leadership or standard of pastoral care. These are the people who say that they did not find the church to be caring or supportive, or that they had found the church's pastoral care to be unprofessional or abusive.

The seventh group left church because they disagreed with the ways in which the church was changing. These are the people who did not like the new hymn books, the new style of worship, the new seating arrangement, or the new minister.

Finally, it is important to note that those who leave the church because they feel the church is too resistant to change are much less likely to return than those who leave the church because the church is too open to change.

## Summary

In this chapter we have re-examined the replies to the 198 statements in our questionnaire concerned with reasons for church leaving in order to address two specific questions. First, we have attempted to sort out the difference between the main precipitating reasons for church leaving and the important but less central predisposing factors. We have suggested that unfulfilled expectations, loss of faith, and the changes and chances of life (like moving home) constitute the main causes associated with church leaving. Second, we have attempted to discover whether individuals who have left churches for some reasons are more likely to consider returning than those who have left for other reasons. We have suggested that church leavers who are most likely to return are those who have left for reasons we have described as changes and chances. These are the people who may have drifted away from the church by default rather than through intention. In a very real sense the churches have been careless in letting such individuals drift away.

# 12   Shaping the Future

One of the encouraging results from our questionnaire survey was to find that church leavers have not necessarily closed the door on future church involvement. When asked 'Are you likely to become actively involved in a church in future?' 45 per cent were leaving the possibility of returning open. This is not to suggest that churches should simply sit back and wait for leavers to return. In this chapter we shall be highlighting a number of important areas for churches to address, if they are serious about wanting to retain their members and to encourage those who have dropped out to return. This cannot be an exhaustive list of remedies for every local situation, but we hope that it will prompt churches to devise strategies of their own.

Knowing *why* certain individuals have left the church can help to shape an appropriate ministry to those individuals. Since it is clear that people leave the church for a variety of different reasons, it is important that pastoral strategy should be responsive to those different reasons. At the same time, if a number of people are leaving the same church for the *same* reason, such information should help the leaders of that church to reflect more deeply on the direction of their ministry.

## Commitment in contemporary society

In chapter one we explored the changing nature of commitment within contemporary society and noted the variety of ways in which Church belonging is understood by different denominations. One of the reasons why people drop out is because there is a mismatch between the degree of commitment they feel able to offer and that expected of them by their Church. Where Church membership categories are too tidy or exclusive, some people may feel alienated. This suggests that there are important ecclesiological questions facing the Church. Is there a place within the Church for the agnostic, the spiritual seeker, the disillusioned, the irregular attender, those who prefer to stay 'on the sidelines', or the morally wayward? Would, for instance, the 'prodigal son' of Jesus' parable be allowed to belong, whilst he remains in 'the far country'? Or is the Church just a tightly bounded community of orthodox Christian believers, living morally transparent lives? Roman Catholic theologian Hans Küng once warned that 'a Church which will not accept the fact that it consists of sinful [people] and exists for sinful [people] becomes hardhearted, self-righteous, inhuman' (Küng 1977:507). Over-rigid Church membership boundaries may fail to reflect the inclusive nature of Christian *koinonia*, as well as actively hamper people's movement towards Christian faith (General Synod Board of Mission 1996:14).

*Youth A Part*, a 1996 Anglican report on young people and the Church, advocated what it termed a 'centred set' approach to Christian belonging, adopted by some of the world's most dynamic and thriving churches. Rather than being unduly concerned about the church's *boundaries* and the need to keep out those who do not conform to accepted standards of belief and behaviour or fail to pull their weight, the 'centred set' model focuses instead on the *centre* of the Church, Jesus Christ. According to the 'centred set' approach, so long as people are moving towards the centre then they can be said to belong. Membership is defined quite loosely and does not necessarily imply prior conformity to a given set of beliefs or values. People are deemed to be members so long as, from whatever direction, they are moving closer in 'biblical knowledge, spiritual growth and commitment to Jesus Christ who is the Centre' (General Synod Board of Education 1996:15). Such an approach to Christian belonging avoids alienating those who feel as yet unable to accept the whole Christian 'package'. As Father Patrick Aikens put it, in an interview in *The Tablet*: 'Is it our job to wave counsels of perfection at people and say, "Achieve this or you are a nobody", or do we put the ideals before people and say, "Go towards them"?'[1]

Our definition of the 'centred set' approach to Church membership does of course presuppose at least a minimal level of Christian belief and practice. But what if people may want to belong, but currently find it impossible to believe? What if people may simply want to turn to their local church for rites of passage – 'hatching, matching and despatching'? It would be misleading to regard such individuals as part of the 'centred set' or the core membership

group, but they may wish to perceive themselves as, in one sense
or another, 'belonging' to the Church. One solution is for Churches
consciously to recognise different types or levels of membership,
encompassing this 'extended family of faith'. People may be
invited to sign up as 'seekers', 'friends of the church', 'associates'
or 'kindred spirits' (Dudley 1979:70,118). In the Methodist Church
anyone in regular contact with the church who is not a Church
member is automatically – whether or not he or she is aware of it –
part of the *Community Roll*. The ideal may be that people eventually
become full Church members, but, in the meantime, churches may
increasingly need to allow people to participate on their own terms,
or risk excluding them altogether.

In a highly mobile society, in which people are linked together
by multiple networks rather than locally based communities, some
Churches may need to consider whether their notion of 'belonging'
is too locally rooted. Is it realistic to expect people to commit
themselves to a single local congregation? Are there adequate
systems to transfer people's membership when they move away?
A young Methodist member recently complained to the *Methodist
Recorder* that she felt 'disenfranchised and disowned' since going
away to university. The local Methodist church, in which she had
grown up, had asked her to reconsider her membership, now she
was living 150 miles away. 'My spiritual home and deepest affinity
remains Methodism [but] for reasons of lifestyle and personal
preference I am reluctant to be bound formally to any one church,'
she said, 'particularly as I have not yet found a community to
which I wish to belong.'[2] A nationally based category of membership might prevent such people becoming part of the statistics of
church decline. The concept of 'local membership' is in any case
difficult to equate with the fact that every Christian is a member
of the Body of Christ and the *universal* Church.

## Dynamics of the leaving process

In chapter two we explored some of the dynamics of the leaving
process. The more that churches understand the process of
leaving, the more they are capable of identifying the warning signs.
The process of leaving does not have to be inevitable or irreversible.
Churches need to be alert for such warning signs as: reduction in
a person's church attendance; mounting alternative pressures on
their time and energy; expressions of disillusionment about the

Christian faith or the church; angry outbursts; emotional distancing and backing away from church friends; increasing attraction of other non-church groups. Individual leavers will not necessarily manifest all of these warning signs, but at least some of these clues may be evident.

One of the most disconcerting findings from our questionnaire survey was that 92 per cent of leavers reported that no one from the church had talked with them about why they were attending church less frequently, during the first six weeks after their church going dropped off. As John Savage's research into United States church leavers found, churches that fail to follow up leavers within six weeks of their leaving are missing an important opportunity. During this period people often passively wait and avoid rein-vesting their time in other organisations. Only if 'no help comes' and no one comes 'to find out why they [have] left' will their departure from the church be finally sealed (Savage 1976:60). Of course some leavers would resent talking about the reasons for their exit. Churches need to show discrimination and sensitivity. Those who have drifted away may get irritated if they are pressed for the 'real reason' why they left (Hadaway 1990:62). Sometimes it may be more appropriate for a church to arrange for a 'neutral' outsider to visit the leaver, on its behalf. One suspects, however, that sometimes churches simply lack the courage and patience to listen seriously to those who might have uncomfortable things to report about their church experience.

Our experience of interviewing church leavers is that people usually much appreciate the opportunity to talk through their reasons for having left. Sometimes the interview takes on a thera-peutic function as leavers express bottled-up hurts and resentments and gain sharper insight into their real motivations for dropping out. Sometimes powerfully positive feelings come to the surface, counter-balancing more negative experiences of the church. Leavers are often deeply impressed that someone has taken the trouble to listen to what they have to say, particularly if that person resists the temptation to jump to the church's defence. Caring, non-judgemental 'exit interviews', that respect the leaver's integrity and sincerity, can play an important part in drawing people back to the church. As a Florida pastor, Stephen Gregory, put it: 'Sudden departures create unfinished business . . . by closing the loop, I leave the door open.'[3] At the very least, talking to leavers can enhance churches' understanding of why people leave.

Ultimately the church's mandate for following up church leavers comes from the gospel itself: what if Jesus had told his hearers this parable?

> Which of you, having a hundred sheep, if you have lost one of them, does not say: 'We can't be bothered to look for strays. We've got a farm to run here! We can't risk the ninety-nine for the sake of just one. If the sheep has gone, it's gone. It's not our fault sheep are silly! We've got other more important things to worry about!' (Altered from Luke chapter 15)

Sadly, some churches give the impression that this is what Jesus actually said, by their relative lack of concern for those who drop out!

## Loss of faith

In chapter three we looked at the role that loss of faith can play in church leaving and identified three main types of atheism: philosophical, experiential and transitional. If churches are to retain their members they need to take account of the difficulties people face in maintaining their faith. Churches need to ask whether they are devoting enough energy to the task of *apologetics*. Are churches taking seriously the actual questions people are asking in late-modern society? Have churches equipped themselves to meet the questions of an increasingly well-educated population? Do churches encourage their members to express doubts and to ask hard-hitting questions? Do churches truly cater for those who are struggling with their faith?

Sometimes local churches can tap into national apologetics initiatives, such as, for example, *The Truth about Science*, a nationwide tour organised by Rob Frost (the Methodist Church's National Evangelist) and David Wilkinson (a Methodist minister and former astrophysicist), in conjunction with the Evangelical Alliance, in 1996–7. Designed as much for the scientifically illiterate as for science graduates, these lively presentations featured prominent scientists facing up to the challenges posed by science to their Christian beliefs.

Churches can also organise local initiatives, maybe as a shared local *Churches Together* project. These could, for instance, take the form of public talks or debates about challenging or controversial topics. Events of this sort can prove to be very popular, especially if well-known speakers can be featured. The ecumenical Christian Centre in Dorking, Surrey, for example, has successfully hosted a series of Spring Lectures during the *Decade of Evangelism*, with such titles as 'Is there anybody there?', 'Why God, Why?', 'What comes next, Lord?', and 'Are you with me, Lord?'

Apologetics is, however, something that every local church needs to address. Do sermons, house-groups, youth work and church bookstalls[4] take the precariousness of people's faith into account? Are there contexts available where people can own up to their doubts and uncertainties in a non-threatening and supportive atmosphere?

It would be a mistake, however, to over-intellectualise the church's response to loss of faith. Sometimes people lose faith because of some trauma or tragedy in their lives, when God seems remote or non-existent. They may feel let down by God when they most need help. This is particularly so if the church, for one reason or another, fails to provide them with adequate pastoral care and support. It is that much more difficult to retain belief in the love of God if this is not concretely reflected in the church's own pastoral care when a person is, for instance, in hospital, made redundant, divorced, bereaved or facing overwhelming family pressures. This suggests that the church that stands alongside people and supports them at times of need is most likely to help people maintain, or retrieve, their faith in the goodness of God. Even those who have lost faith and left their church behind may still request its services at times of profound transition in their lives, when they get married, when they become a parent, when they lose a loved one. These are important opportunities for churches. As people come face to face with the mysteries of love and life and death they may find their fascination with the transcendent rekindled, especially if the loving compassion of God shines through in their experience of the church on these occasions.

Where people have doubts or have virtually lost their faith it is important that churches affirm the faith that people have, however vestigial that may be. People may need to be reassured that doubt is not the enemy of faith. Faith entails living with uncertainty and it is apathy, rather than doubt, that is the opposite of faith. As St Augustine put it: '*Si comprehendis, non est Deus*' (anything your intellect is able to comprehend is too small to be God). Churches are perhaps not as good as they might be at giving out the message that it is OK to attend church in the hope of rediscovering faith. A few months before his conversion in 1738 John Wesley received paradoxical, but ultimately timely, advice from a Moravian Christian called Peter Böhler. Wesley was concerned at his own lack of faith and had almost decided to leave off preaching. Böhler's advice was to 'preach faith *till* you have it; and then, *because* you have it, you *will* preach faith'.[5]

It may well be appropriate for people with severe religious doubts to receive the Eucharist. As Father Allan White, Catholic Chaplain at Cambridge University, put it, when commenting on Catholic lapsing: 'Communion is not like prizegiving. It's food for travellers. It's medicine.'[6] Methodists have traditionally seen the Eucharist as 'a converting ordinance', not just for those in a state of grace. Some churches would of course find this much too open and accommodating and prefer to set strong doctrinal entry-standards. Unfortunately, in the process, they might accelerate the departure of those who are unsure of their faith. The church epitomised in the words of a senior Anglican bishop may be of much greater help: 'Ours has been an untidy Church where a lot of people in the pews can call themselves atheists but they still do belong.'[7]

## Cultural change

In chapter four we explored some of the cultural differences affecting church leaving, especially between those who have been born since 1945 and those who are older. Churches often blithely blame the 'generation gap' for their declining memberships, but do very little homework to identify the cultural differences that, for instance, characterise Baby Boomers (born between 1945 and 1960) and Baby Busters (born between 1961 and 1981), or the various youth sub-cultures.

According to our research, Baby Boomers are leaving churches because they find them to be too much like other institutions and lacking authenticity and credibility; they reject 'pre-packaged' religion; they find churches too dogmatic and conformist; they sense that their values and lifestyle are not welcome at church; they feel stunted by the church in their spiritual and personal growth; and they look in vain for their church to be genuinely concerned for wider social and global issues. Baby Busters have extra reasons for leaving churches: they resent being treated as passive consumers; they reject easy answers and any hint of manipulation; and they find that worship is too intellectualised and fails to engage all their senses. There is no need simply to take our word about these cultural reasons for church leaving. It would be a useful exercise for any local church to invite a panel of Boomer, and/or Buster, church leavers to talk about the specific things in the church which make people of their generation cringe. It would also be worth hearing the things they most appreciate about the church, since they may not have written it off altogether!

Churches do not necessarily have to become experts in analysing cultural change. Local church leaders, lay and clergy, may simply need to listen more intently and empathetically to their own children and grandchildren. As the writers of *Youth A Part* perceptively noted: 'if young people are taken seriously, respected and truly valued, the "gap" between Church culture and youth culture will decrease and close quite naturally' (General Synod Board of Education 1996:22). As far as possible, it is important for churches to affirm youth culture and Boomer and Buster values. Little purpose is served by drawing up battle lines between the generations. In fact new generations often have a habit of saying things that the church needs to hear. Those who have dropped out may turn out to be prophets, calling the church to rediscover its own essence. How far is there a ring of truth about their criticisms? What common ground can be recognised between the values of the church and the values of these leavers? A church that is energetically concerned for the environment, that actively seeks and embodies a more just and caring society, or that offers practical opportunities for people to grow spiritually and personally, is not only likely to be more authentically Christian, but also to be more attractive to Baby Boomers, many of whom rightly continue to place a high premium on such things.

This is not to suggest, however, that the church should merely endorse the cultures with which it engages. It will invite fellow travellers to voyage further and to transcend elements of their own culture. Like the Boomers, the church is interested in promoting 'self fulfilment', but not that of the self-centred grasping ego, nor a selfish quest for happiness. Churches must enhance and deepen, as well as affirm, cultural values.

One of the key responses churches could make to the cultural changes we have explored is to increase the diversity of their programmes, especially their diet of worship. Today's religious consumers appreciate variety of choice and the freedom to select their own style of faith. Personal pilgrimage, rather than pre-packaged faith, is the order of the day. This does not mean that churches need to shut down all their present activities and start something radically new. Rather, they could do with imaginatively supplementing what is already there, to give people maximum freedom of choice. Diversity is, after all, integral to the original vision of the Christian Church (1 Corinthians 12:14–27). Many churches are already experimenting with 'alternative' or 'complementary' styles of worship, sometimes very successfully and creatively. Perhaps the least successful approach nowadays is to try to blend every cultural taste into a single main worship service, which offers enough of each worship style to alienate its opponents but insufficient to please its advocates!

There are four other main options: services based on separate church communities, services based in specific congregations, special celebrations, or 'pilgrimages'. The first option entails setting up a new church community, committed to alternative worship, such as the Late Late Service in Glasgow. The second option is to have separate congregations meeting for alternative worship at times other than the church's main worship service, encouraged to be culturally relevant and semi-autonomous, but remaining within the overall ambit of the local church. One such example is The Warehouse at York. The third option is to hold alternative worship 'celebrations' (sometimes one-off events, sometimes more regular), either locally or on a larger scale. These are typically aimed primarily at young people, one example being Cutting Edge, a quarterly event in the Colchester area. The fourth option is to offer the chance to visit places of pilgrimage, such as Taizé or Iona, or annual festivals, such as Greenbelt, Spring Harvest or Easter People. Such 'pilgrimages' may well cross-fertilise the life and worship of the local church. It is not inconceivable that large churches might one day emulate the multiplex approach of the modern cinema with its multiplicity of 'screens' under the same roof, catering simultaneously for different preferences.

There is no such thing as a 'typical' alternative service. Each tends to reflect the creativity and inspiration of a particular group. Services cannot simply be borrowed in their entirety from else-where; worship is the 'heart-language' of the people of God in a given place and time (Wright 1994:56). Some features, however, tend to recur, such as: the crossing of needless cultural barriers; communication that transcends the spoken word; holistic engagement of body, mind and soul; the use of electronic multi-media technology; stimulation of all the senses; eclectic borrowing from a variety of spiritual traditions; the invitation to participate, rather than passively spectate; an attitude of reverence for, and enjoyment of, the life of this planet. Alternative worship often has the knack of allowing those who are culturally alienated by the Church the space to find their way back. As a *Greenbelt* writer put it: 'There appear to be a lot of "walking wounded" Christians, who don't want anything to do with the Church, or are hanging on to their faith, but only just, who find alternative worship groups a safe place to be.'[8]

Churches do, of course, need to consider how to overcome certain of the risks associated with some experimental types of worship, but since when was risk-taking not associated with Christianity? Is there, for instance, a danger of forming a satellite that spins out of control? Are the leaders properly accountable? Might doctrinal purity be sacrificed on the altar of cultural relevance? Are the financial costs likely to spiral? Could the raising of resources for such events compromise the church's stance on other issues? For example, one country parish in Surrey has started to market its own 'Dog Collar' brand of real ale to try to cover the costs of its alternative youth-oriented services, which include 'video projections [and] sound and light systems, along with drama'.[9] Might it burn out its leaders? Could it split the Body of Christ on an ageist basis? Might those who choose not to attend begin to be classed as 'second-class' Christians? Is it just a gimmick, that people will see through? Experimental worship comes in different forms – from circle dancing to charismatic prayer ministry, from Celtic spirituality to multi-media, multi-sensory raves. Some forms are closer to a particular church's ethos than others. Churches sometimes lack the necessary resources to stage alternative worship. It is worth remembering, however, that as well as looking for cultural relevance Boomers and Busters respect churches that simply impress them as authentic and transparent to the gospel (Roof and Gesch 1995:75).

## Journey of faith

In chapter five we highlighted the importance of understanding and respecting people's faith journeys. The church that is best at retaining its members is one that presupposes that individuals grow in faith, in their own time and in their own way. It knows that people will be at different stages in their faith journeys and does not try to force them into a stage of faith above or below their own. It takes special care of those in transition between different stages of faith and even allows people the freedom to 'outgrow' the church and to have a 'faith sabbatical' (General Synod Board of Mission 1996:11), at least for the time being. One particular group of people worth focusing on is students in higher education, often experiencing the no man's land between stages three and four in James Fowler's model of faith development. It is surely a retrograde step for Churches to be reducing their chaplaincy provision as is the case in many universities at present.

One way of preventing people from dropping out is for churches to respond positively to their desire to grow in faith. Churches might consider offering one of a number of courses that are currently available. They will need to be aware, however, that some of these courses are less to do with faith journeying and more to do with instruction in *the* faith. A given course may not be relevant to all faith stages.

Perhaps the best-known of these courses is *Alpha*, pioneered by Holy Trinity Brompton, which has had extraordinary appeal. It was claimed in 1997 that over 4,500 *Alpha* Courses were running in Britain, in almost every denomination, and that, worldwide, 120,000 people were estimated to be involved each week.[10] Designed to be a practical introduction to Christian faith, *Alpha* takes place over a course of ten sessions. In each session, after a light meal, there is a talk about a central aspect of Christian faith, based on clear, user-friendly *Alpha* teaching materials and videos, and then the opportunity to talk in small groups. The course also includes a weekend away, focusing on the Holy Spirit. *Alpha* culminates in a celebration supper party. Although primarily designed for newcomers to Christianity, churches have also found it useful as a refresher course for the already committed. *Alpha* has been very popular, but churches should be aware that they are using a charismatic evangelical product, reflecting a particular theology of the Holy Spirit. The course is copyrighted and cannot be adapted or altered in any way that changes 'the essential nature of the course'. For people who prefer not to have their faith 'prepackaged' in this way there are other alternatives worth exploring.

*Emmaus*, a course published jointly by the Bible Society and the National Society/Church House Publishing presents Christian faith as an ongoing 'process of discovery' in which 'there is no point at which we can say we have "arrived" '. The course takes the form of 'an accompanied journey'. Whilst it is group-centred it allows people to go at their own pace. The 'nurture' stage of the course is designed to enable people to explore the Christian faith, prior to confirmation or adult baptism, in fifteen flexible sessions. This leads on to the 'growth' stage of the course, continuing the faith journey and exploring how it 'affects... whole lives and the life of the whole church'. *Emmaus* recognises that faith need not stop growing at confirmation. This is a much less prescriptive course than *Alpha* and one that is not simply designed for initial enquirers.

A similar approach, focusing as much on the *process* of discovery as on *content*, is offered by the Roman Catholic *Rite of Christian Initiation of Adults* (*RCIA*). This has also been successfully used outside the Roman Catholic context by, for instance, Anglican churches in the dioceses of Portsmouth and Sheffield. The Roman Catholic diocese of Nottingham has recently produced a resource book, based on the *RCIA*, called *God for Grown-ups*, which invites users to explore the 'Christian story' alongside their own 'personal story'.

Then there is the *Catechumenate Network* which similarly sees growth in faith in terms of exploration, rather than instruction. A *Catechumenate* group begins by establishing bonds of trust between group members. It then listens to, and addresses, the issues that really matter to people in the group. Unlike the *Alpha* Course, the agenda is set by the enquirers, rather than the leaders.[11]

Some courses are more content-based. *Disciple*, published by the Methodist Publishing House, is an ambitious thirty-four week course, during which participants read 70 per cent of the Bible. Based on North-American materials, study groups commit themselves to meeting for two-and-a-half hours each week. The aim is to deepen people's Christian discipleship by thorough immersion in Bible study.

*Credo*, by contrast, is for those still at the enquiry stage. *Credo* is a seven-week course, identifiably Anglo-Catholic in emphasis, structured around the themes of the Creed. The accent is on instruction and teaching input is available on video, although leaders are free to present material in their own way.[12]

As we have seen, there is a variety of courses available. Some have fixed, non-negotiable contents, others are more adaptable to

denominational needs. Some encourage an open-ended, exploratory approach, others dictate a set syllabus. Some are designed for
initial enquirers, others are suitable for people later on in their
journey of faith. The more didactic courses may best suit those at
an early stage in their faith development. Churches may choose to
select the best elements from several courses. The conviviality and
bonding encouraged by *Alpha's* meals and weekend away could
be combined with *Emmaus'* less prescriptive and more liberal
approach, for instance.

Courses like these are a good way of focusing a church's attention on people's need to grow in their faith journey. Some people,
however, will steer clear of courses, suspecting that they will be
too formal or directive. Churches could do with exploring other
alternatives, especially for people at later stages of faith development. A non-directive, no-holds-barred, discussion forum along the
lines of Holy Joe's (see chapter 5) is one possible model. Another
possibility would be to promote church versions of the 'reading
groups' that are popular in the United States – informal social
gatherings where people meet to discuss a given book. Such
reading groups need not confine themselves to narrowly 'religious'
books and could, for instance, explore religious themes in a contemporary novel or discuss the implications of the book *The State
We're In*, by Will Hutton (1996), for Christian social action. Whatever route a church chooses to take, it is important that it offers
people opportunities to grow in their faith and to respect the faith
journeys of others, if that church is to retain its members and
attract leavers to return.

It is a worthwhile exercise for churches to stand back occasionally from their busy programmes and to ask whether they are
genuinely taking account of people's different faith journeys. Are
sermons or church newsletters, for instance, catering successfully
for seekers as well as the already-converted, for experienced as
well as 'nearly-new' Christians? Are they engaging with people at
different stages in the journey of faith and gently encouraging
their development? How far is the continued faith development of
clergy and lay leaders a priority? A growing church is a church
that takes seriously people's growth in faith.

## Changes and chances

In chapter six we focused on the effects on church leaving of life's changes and chances. Churches are most likely to retain their members through the changes and chances of life if, first, they don't allow milestones to become millstones and, secondly, they are prepared to redefine 'problems' as 'opportunities'.

People are most likely to stay with a church that stays alongside them at the important milestones in their lives. Some churches could do with developing a sharper focus on these areas. Does the church, for instance, take enough care of people when they move house? Does it ensure that those moving away are put in touch with a church in their new neighbourhood? Does it make newcomers welcome, without overwhelming them? Does it provide 'welcome packs' to introduce people to the church and local area? Might it offer people the chance to have their new home blessed?

Could the church offer more support to people facing particular life-changes, such as marriage, parenthood, redundancy, retirement or divorce?[13] It might, for example, consider running support groups for parents of pre-school children or teenagers, enabling parents to share their parenting dilemmas in a mutually supportive atmosphere. It could organise special seminars on such issues as 'marriage enrichment' or 'enjoying your retirement' or 'coping with divorce' or 'money management'. The church's Sunday worship might need to be more in touch with the actual changes and chances affecting people. What are the blind spots in the prayers of intercession? Might people appreciate the opportunity for silent personal prayer in which they can express their true hopes and fears? The more that people's actual experience of life is given sense and healing by the church, the more people will be prepared to keep with the church, come what may.

It is important to avoid getting into the mindset whereby all the changes and chances of life are perceived as 'problems' for a person's church going. Old age, whilst it may bring poorer health and less mobility, gives people more spare time to be involved in the church. The awareness that human life does not go on for ever can stimulate a renewed interest in the spiritual dimension. Old age presents the church with new opportunities, as well as challenging problems. Parenthood, as we have seen, can make people more likely to return to church or, at least, to make sure that their children have the opportunity of going to church. It is important for churches to open up non-threatening and welcoming lines of communication with the parents of children in their junior church (Sunday school) and church-related youth organisations. Mid-life crisis can, on the one hand, disrupt a person's church going habits but, on the other hand, may stimulate renewed interest in the church on the part of those who have lapsed. As *Newsweek* noted in 1994, Baby Boomers, many of whom are presently in their forties, are now in the 'contemplative afternoon of life': they 'face the inevitable: neither jogging nor liposuction nor all the brown rice in China can keep them young forever'; increasingly aware of their own mortality, 'they are at a point in their lives where they sense the need for spirituality'.[14] Churches need to be alert to the new opportunities, as well as the obstacles, presented by life changes.

With a little imagination and creativity, even the dramatic social changes that have affected the way people spend Sunday could be treated as exciting new opportunities. If current service times are inconvenient, churches could decide on new times or develop services at other times in the week. If children are no longer coming to junior church because of their parents' new Sunday shopping habits, then churches could follow the example of the Salvation Army at Maidstone in Kent which, in spite of its opposition to Sunday trading, has successfully collaborated with its local Tesco branch to offer Sunday school activities at the supermarket.[15]

## Childhood

In chapter seven we noted that the seeds of church leaving can be set during childhood. If parents, or step-parents, do not attend church regularly this sets a negative example for their children. Equally, parents who are over-committed to the church, or over-keen to get their children involved, can unintentionally stifle their children's church going. It is hard for families to learn the art of transmitting a love of church going to the next generation. There are many powerful influences in contemporary society outside the family's control, but families can still offer children their earliest and most deep-seated experience of Christian community and church going. Families need all the support that churches can offer them in this vital, but often very lonely, task, given the isolated nature of the modern nuclear family.

If church leaving is to be prevented, churches need to ask themselves whether they are 'family-friendly'. For instance, does the church programme genuinely cater for all age groups? Is the church accessible to pushchairs? What happens if a young parent needs to change a nappy or to breast-feed? Is there a 'toddlers' club' to give a respite to harassed parents? Could the church offer 'after-school clubs' for 'latch-key' children, if both parents need to work? Are church youth organisations sufficiently sensitive to the financial barriers to full involvement faced by children from poorer families?

Do families have the chance to be together in church? Churches are often very good at providing separate activities for individual members of the family but, strangely, sometimes forget that families also appreciate and benefit from doing things together. It is true that family mealtimes may have given way nowadays to independent 'grazing', but there remain activities, such as a day out at a theme park, that many families enjoy doing together. Such events become especially significant and memorable because the whole family has participated, albeit to varying levels of terror! Maybe nowadays it is the family that *plays* together that stays together? Does the church encourage its families also to *pray* together in its Sunday worship or are children always shepherded off elsewhere for their own activities? Children's experience of church may be often limited to experience of junior church. Is it surprising if they find it impossible to make the transition from junior church to adult church going? It is good for children to have the experience of going to church with the rest of their family. This is especially important at the main Christian festivals, but needs to happen regularly at other times of the year too, if parents' church going is to rub off on to their children.

Parenting is not easy in today's complex and often bewildering society. Without being too intrusive or directive, could not churches offer parents some insights into effective parenting? The church programme could include a 'parenting course'. Many churches have successfully used the excellent course material produced by the Family Caring Trust.[16] The church bookstall could include titles dealing with the practicalities of parenting. The entertaining paperback, *The Sixty Minute Father*, by Rob Parsons (1995), for instance, is well worth considering. The book is designed to be read in just sixty minutes and to help fathers make time to become better parents. Churches could also encourage the formation of parent mutual support groups, to enhance people's confidence and skills in parenting.

There is no such thing, in reality, as the 'ideal family'. In most churches families will come in varying shapes and forms. Some will be childless families. Some will be mum and dad and 2.4 children. Some children will have extra parents, because their parents have remarried. Some children will have lost parents. Some family members will live on their own. It is important that churches do not set discouragingly high ideals. As David Gamble, Family and Personal Relationships Secretary in the Methodist Church, has put it: 'I believe Christians should accept this [diversity] and support people as they try their best. We need to affirm the good rather than always point to the bad.'[17]

It is important that churches not only promote good parenting but also allow people the space and time to be good parents. Churches could do with carefully monitoring the demands they place on parents. Is it more important to have all the jobs in the church filled or to have parents who can spend quality time with their children? In the long run the survival of the church may depend more on good parenting than on good office holding!

## Cost of church involvement

In chapter eight we looked at the 'costs' of church involvement and at some of the factors that can lead church leavers to decide that their investment is too costly. We found that some people leave churches because they have become 'burned out' by excessive demands on their time, energy or money. Others resent the presence of 'free riders' who do not properly pull their weight. We concluded that people are less likely to treat a church as a 'lost cause' when it is seen to be focused in its life and mission.

It is important that churches do not overload their members. People's commitment to their church has to be held in balance with their family responsibilities, work pressures and recreational needs. At some times in their lives it may be unrealistic and insensitive to expect individuals to have the time and energy to help run their local church. Churches often unthinkingly 'twist people's arms' to help, and risk either overburdening individuals or inspiring inappropriate guilt among those who cannot make themselves available. Churches could do with monitoring the burdens they expect their lay leaders to carry. Are all the jobs necessary? Do people serve for a fixed term and have the opportunity to stand down before they get burned out? Does the church make full use of those with fewer 'outside responsibilities', such as those who have retired early or the elderly?

One way of preventing burnout is to involve lay people only in tasks for which they have actively volunteered. Instead of continually trying to persuade people to fill jobs for which they may be unsuited, and risking 'square pegs in round holes', some churches simply advertise a set of volunteering options. Frazer Memorial United Methodist Church in Montgomery, Alabama, for instance, a church of some 7,500 members, offers a 'Ministry Menu' every November of nearly two hundred options for getting involved in some form of lay ministry. When people tick items on the menu they offer themselves for just one year, although they are free to renew their commitment the following year. They are also free to suggest and volunteer for new lay ministries. If no one volunteers for a particular task then this may be taken as a sign that this particular ministry has come to the end of its natural life. Frazer's senior pastor, John Ed Mathison, believes that this 'menu-driven' approach has significant advantages: 'When people volunteer for a task, they have greater ownership, with greater follow-through [and] greater performance and excellence. The volunteer system takes advantage of people's strongest interests, and it affirms their talents and giftedness' (Mathison 1988:21–2). The more that people are free to volunteer for tasks within the church that meet their needs and gifts, the less burnout is likely to be experienced.

If a church is serious about its core beliefs and has a contagious vision of where it is going, people are more willing, in the words of Studdert-Kennedy's hymn: 'to give and give and give again what God has given thee, to spend thyself nor count the cost, to serve right gloriously'.[18] Church leaving is less likely when a church captures and shares a driving vision of what it is about. That God-given vision can be inspired and reinspired from many different sources, such as prayer, the Scriptures, inspirational leadership, stories of what has made a particular denomination or congregation 'tick' in the past,[19] or the onset of a deep human need or injustice in the community at large that draws out the church's response. The decline of mainstream churches, according to Carl Dudley, has been less to do with 'doing too little or too much [of] the wrong thing', than with churches seeming 'to forget why they are doing anything' and losing their 'vision of Jesus Christ as Lord of the whole world' (Dudley 1979:83). The prevention of church leaving has as much to do with a recovery of that sense of vision as the adoption of specially crafted strategies.

One way of identifying and encapsulating the vision of any given local church is for it to write its own mission statement. What exactly does this church exist to be and do? Who does the church exist for? What are its core values? What can other people expect from the church? How does it hope to develop in the future? The best mission statements are written and owned by the whole church community, not just its leadership. They are intended to excite and inspire people, both within and beyond the church, with a contagious vision of what the church is about.

## Unfulfilled expectations of the church

In chapter nine we looked at the role that people's unfulfilled expectations of the church can play in church leaving. People are not always able to forgive the church for failing to live up to their dreams. When they see no prospect of the church changing or are fazed by changes they dislike, they can become disillusioned and drop out.

Churches cannot and should not hope to please everyone. Some people's expectations are out of line with Scripture and tradition, but it would be a worthwhile exercise for churches to take stock now and then and actually check with their members to see how far their legitimate expectations are being met. This could take place in the context of a specially called synod or assembly. The Bible Society offers an excellent *Consultancy* service, which can help churches reappraise their values and goals. A simple questionnaire or 'audit' could be devised by a local church to explore members' expectations of worship, pastoral care, leadership and teaching.[20] Churches may well find the results encouraging, as well as challenging. It is vital, however, that this is not just an exercise in gathering opinions or statistics, but also designed to shape the church's forward strategy. People are more likely to stick with a church that is genuinely responsive to their ideals.

People may take some convincing that the church can change and become more authentic. This is particularly the case after they have left. As one teenager put it to us: 'A lot of people, once they've left, they see [the church] as going to stay the same, so they just don't bother trying it any more. They just think that it's always going to be boring, so they don't come back.' The 'Classic

FM effect' should, however, give some grounds for hope. Who would have imagined, a decade ago, that classical music could be made 'sexy'? Against all the odds, 'Classic FM' has succeeded in changing the image of classical music. The same could be achieved for the church's image! If people who have dropped out of church 'could be persuaded that it's getting better, they'll come back', predicted another teenage interviewee.

The message for ex-church goers might need to sound something like this: 'Come back to church, to your roots, and check us out for yourselves. Church has changed since you were here last, you may not recognise it. Don't ask us why it's taken so long to get our act together and we won't ask you where you've been!'[21]

How can a church convince people that it is willing to change and to take their dreams seriously? It can start by involving as many people as possible in its decision-making. It can try to make sure that no one feels marginalised. Young people, in particular, need to sense that their voice counts and that they can have a role in bringing about change. Older people, often quite unintentionally, tend to be good at patronising the young. Wouldn't it be good for churches to ban phrases such as: 'You're too young to understand!' or 'We tried that once, but it didn't work!'? Why shouldn't older people have to justify their standpoints, as well as the young? Who is to say that those who are older have necessarily progressed further in the journey of faith? Young people are less likely to be alienated from the church if older people treat them as 'brothers and sisters in Christ', and as equal partners whose dreams for the church are no less important than their own.

Churches should certainly not be in the business of 'dream busting'. If someone has an idea for something new in which the church might be involved, and this is not out of step with the church's theology or ethos, why not let them give it a try? Even if similar ideas have failed in the past, this could now be the right time and the right person for the idea to succeed. As Rick Warren, pastor of Saddleback Valley Community Church in California, put it: '[Even] if the idea seems screwball, it is better to let them find it out than for you to tell them ... If you are the dream buster – telling people their idea won't fly – pretty soon your people quit trying!' (Hunter 1996:139)

Some people, of course, are not looking for change. They would prefer things to stay as they are. For their sake, churches need to manage necessary changes sensitively. It is all too easy to alienate people by hasty, autocratic changes. Take, for example, a leadership that wants to change the time of the main Sunday service. How might unnecessary conflict be avoided over such an issue? First and foremost, a process of genuine consultation is vital. People need to be confident that their opinions matter and that the leadership will not simply dictate 'what's best'. Where discussion becomes heated, it is important to list the pros and cons of alternative service times as dispassionately and fairly as possible. Is a compromise solution possible? Sometimes people are simply afraid of the new and would be reassured if the proposed changes were tried out for an experimental period. It is important to take into account the powerful memories that may be associated with whatever one is trying to change. If, for instance, someone is implacably opposed to replacing the church's pews with moveable chairs, it is worth considering what the pews represent for that person: might it be possible to reincorporate some of the wood elsewhere in the church? As far as possible, churches need to avoid manoeuvring people into tight corners, from which their only way of saving face is to leave the church.

## Need to belong

In chapter ten we explored people's need for a sense of belonging and the variety of ways in which this could be expressed. Any church that wants to hold on to its members must take its community-building vocation seriously. From a sociological perspective, for a person to have a sense of belonging to any community three things are necessary: shared beliefs and values; frequent interaction; and mutual social support and aid (Hornsby-Smith 1992:127).

It is not enough for a church simply to presume that its members share a common core of *beliefs and values*. It must provide opportunities for those beliefs and values to be nourished and celebrated. Although healthy churches always leave room for disagreement and constructive criticism, they are also clear about what they live for – and would die for. Ironically, sermons are sometimes not the best guide to the church's core beliefs and values. Preachers often 'preach to the converted' and simply presuppose that their listeners know what the church stands for! People often perceive the heart of what the church is about in a small-group setting where they have the confidence to ask questions. Sometimes it is helpful to go away on retreat or pilgrimage, so that, at a distance, one can 'see the wood for the trees' and identify the beliefs and values that really matter. This could be anything from a church weekend-away to a pilgrimage to Iona or Lourdes or an event such as Greenbelt or Spring Harvest.

*Frequent interaction* is also vital for a sense of belonging. People are unlikely to feel that they belong if their only contact with the church is for an hour each Sunday, however user-friendly and welcoming that church happens to be. People are most likely to stay if they form friendship networks within the church that carry over to the rest of the week. One way of encouraging this is to invite people to belong to small groups of various kinds. It is important to offer a variety of groups, from Bible study to banner-making. One need not be embarrassed that such groups have a social dimension. It is OK for people to come to Bible studies for the home-made cakes afterwards as well as for the meat of holy Scripture! It is important to remember that small groups will not suit everyone. Some men, for instance, may be willing to take part in a task-oriented group, but not a group which expects them to 'bare their soul'. They may be happy to be involved in a soup-run for the homeless, but less keen on a prayer group.

*Mutual support and aid* also promote a sense of belonging. It is easier for people to feel that they belong to the church community if they sense a caring atmosphere and realise that here are others that they can trust and turn to if the going gets tough. Again, small groups can play an important part in developing the caring, supportive relationships every church needs. It is important that the church's 'rhetoric of caring' is translated into practical acts of caring, when a person needs it most. Churches need to check, from time to time, whether people actually rate them as caring communities. Do some people slip through the net? Does the church have particular blind spots? Is there a good network of communication so that pastoral carers know when they are most needed?

In today's increasingly mobile society, when people do not always stay very long in a locality, churches need to find ways of accelerating the growth of trust and mutual caring between their members. In a more static society there is time for this to happen naturally. Nowadays such a process may need a little help. One of the attractions of *Alpha* has been the intensity of interaction built into the course, in the form of small-group discussion, meals and a weekend away. Church outings and holidays can also be very effective ways of speeding up the development of a sense of community.

It is important for churches to offer people a sense of community, but not just any sort of community. Churches sometimes settle for a cosy, close-knit version of community, most closely resembling a traditional village. Unfortunately, village-style communities may often be preoccupied with themselves, they may be slow to welcome strangers, they may mercilessly stereotype their members, and they may be claustrophobic places in which to live. The church, on the other hand, if it is to incarnate the values of God's kingdom, will be an outward-looking community, hospitable towards strangers, affirmative of others, and offering room to breathe and grow. Churches need to consider carefully what type of community they are offering. Is the person who prefers anonymous, cathedral-style worship catered for? Is it easy for newcomers to find their way in? Are the clergy simply chaplains to the church community, ministering to the needs of its members, or truly engaging with the life of the world and, as Studdert-Kennedy once put it, daring to live 'within a yard of hell'?

Ideally, the sense of community offered by the church should go well beyond that offered elsewhere. The church's mandate is to be a radically inclusive community, in which divisions of colour, race, class, sex, gender, nationality and physical or mental ability no longer make people feel excluded. Churches could do with regularly monitoring how far they are putting that vision into practice. Maybe the church's leadership is top-heavy with white indigenous males? Maybe there is inadequate wheelchair-access to the church?

Nowadays, people's friendship networks, leisure interests and working lives may take them far away from the neighbourhood in which they reside. Churches need to be realistic about the degree of involvement people can have in the activities of their local church. Equally, however, this is an opportunity for the church's understanding of itself to be deepened. The church, after all, is the *People of God*, who do not stop being the church, Monday to Friday, in their many different walks of life. Churches need to ask themselves whether they are effectively supporting the laity in their various vocations. Does anyone actively help them to relate their faith and their everyday work? Unless what happens at church is relevant to the rest of a person's life they may not feel they still belong to the church once they leave its doors.

Human beings are created with a hunger for community that is not met by a society that is often individualistic, anonymous and brutal. Churches keep alive a radically different vision of human togetherness. Not surprisingly, some people return to church going because they eventually realise that they 'cannot go it alone' and that the church has something unique to offer. The more that churches truly mirror the community of love at the heart of the universe – Father, Son and Holy Spirit – the more people will want to go on belonging.

## Conclusion

To sum up, churches are most likely to retain their members and encourage leavers to return when they:
- avoid pigeon-holing people into tidy membership categories;
- notice and react sensitively when people are leaving;
- avoid blowing out any embers of faith;
- meet and respect people where they are culturally;
- meet and respect people where they are spiritually;
- help people grow in their faith;
- offer practical support as people cope with life's changes and chances;
- encourage parents in their upbringing of children;
- offer people a gospel worth investing in;
- authentically embody the gospel;
- offer people a sense of true community.

In this chapter we have explored some ideas and examples of good practice that can help churches hold on to their members and encourage leavers to return. These suggestions are not intended to make churches feel guilty about what they are failing to do, instead they are designed to enhance and focus what is already being done in many places. These suggestions are also by no means narrowly confined to church leaving: many are just as relevant to the church's wider mission and will help encourage people through the church's front door.

There is no one magic solution to the problem of church leaving. As we have seen, churches need to consider a cocktail of remedies, because people drop out of church for a whole variety of reasons. Why not experiment with a range of responses? Church back doors might then start to become redundant!

# A Parable

Imagine that your idea of a perfect holiday was to take an organised coach tour, lasting several days, somewhere on the British mainland. Over the years you had become a regular customer, like your parents in times past. Your mother and father had passed on their own enthusiasm for coach tours and you looked back fondly to those on which you had been taken in your youth. Sadly your parents' enthusiasm had had quite the opposite effect on your younger brother, who now studiously avoided holidays of this sort. Your own liking for coach tours had been reinforced by the good friends you had made on holiday over the years.

But then things had begun to change. Your last holiday was just a little too expensive and you felt it did not really offer value for money. It certainly did not live up to what the brochure had led you to expect. The coach party was not nearly as friendly as before. Cliques formed and you had felt excluded. You had already, for some time, started to entertain doubts about whether to go on any more coach tours. This holiday clinched it. In fact your very idea of a perfect holiday had begun to change. At your time of life and with your work pressures a holiday lazing in the sun on a tropical beach became irresistible. Coach tours were just too regimented and you felt the need for more independence. It began to dawn on you that all through your life you had been copying your parents' holiday habits.

The time had come to take the opportunity to do your own thing. You could be more adventurous – a holiday in the sun this year, a fortnight backpacking in the Himalayas next year. . . . And wouldn't it be good for you to have a weekend at a health farm? The idea of taking another coach holiday was not entirely ruled out, but only if it was your choice and in any case not for the time being.

# Appendix:  Methodology

## Introduction

There are two main methods of undertaking sociological surveys –
the *quantitative* approach and the *qualitative* approach. As the name
implies, the quantitative approach involves the collection of statistical data. Providing the group of people surveyed has been
randomly selected and is sufficiently large and representative, and
providing there is a reasonable response rate, it is possible to
generalise with some certainty from the survey's findings. News-
papers, for instance, will often adopt this approach when they want
to report on people's voting intentions. Inevitably, the quantitative
approach cannot do complete justice to the richness and complexity
of people's behaviour. It deals with people *en masse*, but there is
no such thing as a perfectly typical human being! For this reason,
the qualitative approach prefers to survey fewer people at much
greater depth. Whilst the quantitative survey will generally use a
series of 'closed' questions, allowing for a limited range of possible
responses, the qualitative survey will typically take the form of
an in-depth guided conversation which, although there may be an
interview guide, may cover quite unexpected territory. Both
approaches have their own strengths and weaknesses: the qualitative approach yields much richer and more nuanced data and
avoids imposing preconceived categories on the material, but lacks
generalisability; the quantitative approach provides a good general
overview, but lacks fine detail.

In the event, we decided to capitalise on the strengths of both
approaches. The first phase of our research adopted a qualitative
approach, involving a series of in-depth interviews with church
leavers and clergy. We defined a church leaver as someone who
has reduced his or her church attendance to less than six times a

year (not including Christmas, Easter, weddings or funerals), having previously attended more frequently than this.[1] On the basis of the themes that emerged from these interviews we were able to develop and refine the questionnaire used in the next phase of the research. In the second phase we adopted a quantitative approach, first, identifying a sample of church leavers in the population at large by means of a random telephone survey and, secondly, inviting their completion of an extensive postal questionnaire.

## Qualitative data

Between 1995 and 1997 we conducted twenty-seven in-depth interviews with a range of people who had left or, in a few cases, switched[2] between Anglican, Roman Catholic, Methodist and 'New Churches'. Sometimes known as 'House Churches' or 'Restorationist Churches', New Churches often meet in hired halls for neo-pentecostalist-style worship. We felt it was important to understand why people dropped out of even these apparently thriving churches and 'fellowships'. All interviewees were encouraged to tell their own stories and to talk in detail about the factors underlying their dropping out.

Our aim was to interview a broad range of leavers from each of the four denominations, especially people within the age groups and gender categories statistically least likely to attend church. We conducted in-depth interviews with fifteen males and twelve females. Nine of our interviewees were Anglican, seven Roman Catholic, seven Methodist, and four were associated with New Churches. Four of our interviewees were in their teens; seven were in their twenties; four were in their thirties; nine were in their forties; and the remaining three were over fifty years old, including one over seventy. The tape-recorded interviews were approximately one hour in length and were subsequently fully transcribed and analysed.

For reasons of economy, most of our interviews took place in the south-east of England. We did, however, conduct two interviews elsewhere in England and four in Northern Ireland. It was not easy to contact church leavers in Northern Ireland, since virtually everyone claims to be a Protestant or a Roman Catholic. We even met the phenomenon of a 'Protestant atheist'! Given the strong political and cultural reasons for church going in Northern Ireland we were especially keen to explore the motivations of those who had defied the tide and dropped out. Although the majority of our interviewees lived in the south-east of England, some had left church earlier in their lives when living elsewhere in the country. Most of our interviewees lived in suburban areas (16), although some lived in the inner city (1), council estates (2), small towns (5) or villages (3). We were keen to set up interviews with members of ethnic minority communities but, in the event, only two in-depth interviews – with a young female of African-Caribbean origin and a young African male – fell into this category.

By definition, church leavers are not the easiest people to contact. Unlike church goers they do not congregate on Sundays with other like-minded people. We considered a number of possible ways of contacting leavers. We ruled out the use of newspaper adverts, inviting leavers to contact us, on the basis that we might simply attract those who had especially strong feelings against the church and who might have a particular 'axe to grind'. We considered contacting those churches that had reported an above average number of leavers in a given year, but concluded that this might be attributable to a single idiosyncratic factor, such as a local scandal or theological disagreement, and that such leavers might not be properly representative. In the end, we decided to contact leavers through the following channels. The majority (17 interviewees) were contacted via clergy. In some cases our contacts with clergy derived from our own personal networks. In most cases, however, clergy were approached on a random basis and invited to co-operate with the survey. We contacted clergy in a range of different types of neighbourhood, whilst excluding any reporting exceptionally high levels of loss, for the reason we have already specified. The help of Churches' national statistical officers was invaluable in helping us to identify these clergy contacts. Other leavers were contacted via university chaplains (2 interviewees), our own contact networks (4 interviewees), 'snow-balling' when further contacts were suggested by our initial contacts (2 interviewees), and a youth group (2 interviewees).

Altogether, over two hundred thousand words were spoken in the interviews. Most of the interviews were conducted in the relaxing and familiar environment of people's own homes. Most people were prepared to speak at considerable depth about their reasons for disengaging from church. We sensed that in some cases this was the first opportunity the interviewee had ever taken to talk about this transition in his or her life. Sometimes the interview appeared to take on a therapeutic function, with tears or verbal violence coming to the surface. In one case, the interviewee found the conversation so personally valuable that she recorded her address and the date at the end of the interview. Several interviewees announced that they would now be giving the church 'another try'.

These twenty-seven in-depth interviews with church leavers were supplemented by nine interviews with eleven clergy, exploring their perceptions of why people leave, and thirty-seven short interviews with Methodist young people attending the Methodist Association of Youth Clubs (MAYC) Weekend in Battersea Park in May 1996. These young people were drawn from all over Britain. Altogether, then, seventy-five individuals were interviewed.

Each interview was tape-recorded, transcribed and analysed in detail by several colleagues. Every interviewee was given an appropriate pseudonym and in some cases personal details were altered, to preserve his or her confidentiality. Adopting a *grounded theory* approach, we found recurrent themes and categories beginning to crystallise from the interview data. These formed the basis for the questionnaire we used in our postal survey. As the reader will notice, some of our interviewees yielded especially rich interview data and it is their accounts on which we focus in this book. One must, naturally, treat the data from these interviews with caution. The interviewees could not always be randomly selected. We generally had to rely on clergy 'gatekeepers' for our contacts. We were, however, able to test out the representativeness of these interviews in our subsequent quantitative survey.

### Quantitative data

During autumn 1996 we conducted a postal survey of church leavers in the general population, using our own extensive questionnaire. As well as eliciting demographic details and information about people's previous church going and disengagement, it included a battery of nearly two hundred possible reasons for their church leaving, to which they were asked to express their agreement or disagreement on a five-point Likert scale (with the following options: 'agree strongly', 'agree', 'not certain', 'disagree' or 'disagree strongly'). The content of the questionnaire was based both on our own qualitative data and also on items from previous surveys, conducted in Britain and the United States. Our questionnaire was designed to be as comprehensive as possible, whilst not exceeding the length of some consumer surveys.

In order to identify a sample of church leavers among the general population, we conducted a random telephone survey which, for reasons of economy, focused on the London area. The primary aim of the survey was to identify 800 individuals living at addresses within the London postal code area, who would be willing to receive postal questionnaires, and who met the following two criteria. The first criterion was that they had once attended any denomination of church at least six times a year (not including Christmas and Easter). The second criterion was that, having attended church at least six times a year, they had subsequently lapsed to less than six times a year. For some, these two criteria meant that currently they were not classified as regular church goers. Others, however, may have resumed regular church attendance after a period of lapsing from attendance.

People were phoned on an entirely random basis. The phone numbers used were taken at regular sampling intervals from the latest edition of the London postal area residential phone book. Altogether 3,567 live calls were made, not including calls to unobtainable numbers and unattended answerphones. Callers were carefully supervised and an automatic computer-log kept of the numbers called. The survey continued until 807 questionnaire recipients had been identified. While 1,499 telephone subscribers declined to take part in the telephone survey, 2,066 agreed to take part. Of these 2,066 telephone interviewees, 1,261 either fell outside the categories in which we were interested or declined to take a questionnaire. A wide social mix was achieved. The only age category that was under-represented was those under twenty years old. The 807 questionnaire recipients comprised 43 per cent males and 57 per cent females, which is quite similar to the sex-ratio of church goers, as measured by the survey undertaken by Brierley (1991) under the title *Prospects for the Nineties* (42 per cent males and 58 per cent females); the percentage in the general population being 49 per cent males and 51 per cent females. It is, perhaps, not surprising that the sex ratio among church leavers should reflect so closely the sex ratio among church goers.

A total of 801 questionnaires were successfully mailed. Thanks to telephone follow-up of tardy respondents we achieved a response rate of 52 per cent. Through the use of a unique reference number on each reply-paid envelope it was possible to log which questionnaires had been returned, whilst preserving complete confidentiality. The questionnaires were coded and analysed using the SPSS statistical package, at Trinity College Carmarthen and University of Wales, Lampeter. Our analysis of the questionnaire data was intended both to map the field of church leaving and also to test out a range of hypotheses deriving from our interview data and the findings of previous studies.

The data from the completed questionnaires make a very significant contribution to our study. It is important, therefore, to say something about the people who responded, in terms of their sex, ages and experience of church going. Two-fifths (40 per cent) of the questionnaires were returned by men and three-fifths (60 per cent) were returned by women. Very few of the respondents (3 per cent) were under the age of twenty, 13 per cent were in their twenties, 17 per cent in their thirties, 23 per cent in their forties, 16 per cent in their fifties, 16 per cent in their sixties, and 13 per cent were aged seventy or over. Among this sample of church leavers, three-fifths (59 per cent) had once attended an Anglican church more than six times a year, one-third (33 per cent) had once attended a Roman Catholic church more than six times a year, and one in eight (13 per cent) had attended a Methodist church more than six times a year. A Baptist church had been attended more than six times a year by 7 per cent of the respondents, a United Reformed Church congregation by 3 per cent, a Salvation Army citadel by 2 per cent, a Society of Friends meeting by 1 per cent, and a New Church fellowship by 1 per cent of the respondents. Other denominations were mentioned by 8 per cent of the respondents. This list of denominations adds up to well over 100 per cent since a number of the respondents had left more than one denomination at different stages in their lives.

### Strengths

Our research, combining both qualitative and quantitative methods, had a number of advantages over previous comparable work. Apart from the study by Michael Fanstone (1993), this was the first major recent study to focus on Britain, rather than the United States. The main survey had no bias towards any particular denomination, unlike, for instance, the work on Catholic dropouts by Dean Hoge (1981) or the work on lapsed United Methodists by John Savage (1976). It combined the best elements of qualitative and quantitative approaches. The survey did not rely solely on the interpretation of statistical data, as had, for example, the delineation of dropouts as 'successful swinging singles', 'sidetracked singles', 'young settled liberals', 'young libertarians' and 'irreligious traditionalists' by C. Kirk Hadaway (1990). Neither was the survey simply verging on the anecdotal, as was, for instance, the study of the unchurched by J. Russell Hale (1977), which lacked adequate 'triangulation' and was largely a single individual's subjective analysis of interview data.

Where we adopted a quantitative approach our approach was rigorously scientific, unlike, one suspects, the study by Fanstone (1993), in which he gives no evidence of having approached people on a random basis; most of his survey participants were located by interviewers in the street 'armed with a clipboard' (p. 52) and he gives no proof that this was a representative sample: the fact that he identified equal numbers of males and females in itself casts doubt on the reliability of the data, given that in church going, females outnumber males. A Gallup Poll conducted for ABC Television in 1964 found that those who no longer regularly attended church comprised 44 per cent men and 56 per cent women (ABC Television 1964:58). Fanstone's questionnaire was also rather too cursory, meaning that some of his final categorisation does not reflect the original set of questions, but is based on the additional comments of just a few respondents (Fanstone 1993:61).

## Summary

In this appendix on methodology we have described the two empirical components of our study, the interviews (designed to generate qualitative data) and the telephone survey and postal questionnaire (designed to generate quantitative data). Inevitably, some church leavers will have slipped through our nets. *Extremely disaffected* people, who still feel very hostile towards the church, and *drifters*, who were never really committed to their church, are less likely to have returned questionnaires or to have agreed to be interviewed. Nevertheless, given that the overall response rate to our main questionnaire was relatively high, we are confident that our nets did not have too many holes.

# Notes

## Introduction

1. *The Financial Times*, 25 March 1996.
2. 'Methodist Church faces "meltdown" ', *The Guardian*, 21 March 1996, p. 12.
3. 'Triennial statistical returns', in *Minutes of Conference and Directory*, London: Methodist Church Conference Office, 1996, pp. 61–70.
4. 'Methodist numbers' (letter from the Secretary of the Methodist Conference), *The Times*, 23 March 1996.
5. 'Catholic church losing mass appeal', *The Guardian*, 30 January 1996, citing figures from the 1996 *Catholic Directory*.
6. *Church Statistics: parochial membership and finance statistics for January to December 1995*, London: The Central Board of Finance of the Church of England, 1997.
7. *The Body Book: 6th Edition*, Romford: Pioneer, 1996, p. 2.
8. We have used the Harvard method for referencing books and journal articles, giving details of the author, date of publication, and page number(s). All books and journal articles cited in this way can be found in the bibliography at the end of the book.
9. The gap between people's claimed and actual levels of church going is, however, probably much less in Britain than in the USA. See Hadaway, Marler and Chaves (1993:749).
10. Robin Gill, 'Practising what the vicar preaches', *Church Times*, 18 April 1997, p. 11.
11. *The Tablet*, 3 May 1997, p. 569.
12. Clifford Longley, 'The "feel-good" factor is going to church', *The Times*, 7 February 1997, p. 29.

## 1. A Retreat from Commitment?

1. These and the following statistics are drawn from Wilkinson and Mulgan (1995:100–101).

2. *The Independent*, 4 January 1997, p. 6.
3. Debi Roker and Katie Player, 'A part of something bigger', *Youth Action*, 60, 1997, p. 11.
4. 'Reaping the profits of tomorrow's world', *The Observer*, 24 November 1996.
5. *Population Trends 85*, London: HMSO, 1996.
6. The Marriage Service, *The Alternative Service Book 1980*, Cambridge: Cambridge University Press, 1980, p. 288.
7. *Communion before Confirmation?* London: CIO Publishing, 1985.
8. *The Methodist Service Book*, Peterborough: Methodist Publishing House, 1975, p. D10.
9. First Communion for children is now becoming part of Anglican practice, following guidelines approved by General Synod in November 1996.
10. The figures are expressed to the nearest whole number.

## 2. The Leaving Process

1. Skonovd (1979), cited in Wright (1988) and as supplemented by Wright (1987).

## 3. No Longer Believing, No Longer Belonging

1. *The Tablet*, 12 August 1995, pp. 1022–3; 19 August 1995, pp. 1050–51, 1043–4.
2. For a critique of Davie's formulation, see Michael Hornsby-Smith (1992).
3. Reported in Abercrombie, Baker, Brett and Foster (1970:106).
4. Cited in Bruce (1995b:425).
5. Cited in Bruce (1995a:51).
6. John H. Westerhoff (1976), cited in Hoge (1981:84).
7. David Hay, 'Religion lacking Spirit', *The Tablet*, 2 March 1996, p. 292.

## 4. Changing Values

1. As we shall see, there are many common themes between Baby Boomers and their successors, Baby Busters.
2. 'John Paul's Critical Mass', *The Observer*, 7 April 1996.
3. 'Opting in and opting out', *The Tablet*, 19 August 1995, p. 1043.
4. 'When believers desert their church', *The Independent*, 23 March 1996.

## 5. Growing into a Different Stage of Faith

1. See, for example, Parks (1992).
2. See, for instance, Ephesians chapter 2.

3. 'Opting in and opting out', *The Tablet*, 19 August 1995, p. 1043.
4. Dave Tomlinson, 'Heralds of Hope?', *Alpha*, September 1996, p. 33.
5. 'Pub open to interpretation', *The Guardian*, 24 August 1996.
6. 'Prophets-of doubt', *Alpha;* August 1996, p. 29.
7. 'Out of the playpen', *The Tablet*, 9 November 1996, pp. 1474–5.
8. *Methodist Recorder*, 18 April 1996, p. 15.

### 6. Changes and Chances

1. The following list is partly based on that of Poore (1992:35).
2. Cited in 'Chapel keeps few friends in the north', *The Independent on Sunday*, 24 March 1996, p. 9.

### 7. Like Parent, Like Child

1. *Wesley's Works*, Sermon XCIV, 'On family religion'.
2. This does not, however, happen today as often as one might expect; see Roozen, McKinney and Thompson (1990:320); see also Roof (1993:165).
3. Parents can, however, be quite selective about the aspects of Christianity to which they want their children to be exposed, preferring just the 'nice bits' (Levitt 1996:128).

### 8. Too High a Cost

1. For a recent treatment of burnout in the church context, see Davey (1995).
2. Methodism is known as the *United Methodist Church* in the United States.
3. Cited in *Asheville Citizen-Times*, 27 August 1995, p. 11A.
4. *Methodist Recorder*, 4 April 1996, p. 17.

### 9. 'Tread softly, for you tread on my dreams'

1. W. B. Yeats, 'He wishes for the Cloths of Heaven'.
2. *Charter '95: A message to The Methodist Church from young people*, MAYC leaflet.
3. Cited in *The Tablet*, 22 February 1997, p. 274.
4. A reference to losses reported by the Church Commissioners in the 1980s.
5. See Dulles (1988).
6. 'Thoughts upon Methodism', in *John Wesley's Works Vol. XIII*, London, p. 260.
7. 'The Church on its knees', *The Sunday Telegraph*, 9 February 1997, p. 22.
8. 'First fill your church', *The Guardian*, 10 February 1997.

9. 'Thrills, spills, lots of fun – but ultimately not real', *The Independent*, 22 February 1997.
10. 'The crossroads', *The Guardian*, 7 December 1995, p. 2.
11. 'The crossroads', *The Guardian*, 7 December 1995, p. 2.
12. Leslie Griffiths, 'Woes of Wesley', *The Tablet*, 6/13 April 1996, p. 470.

## 10. Believing but not Belonging

1. Revd Dr Robinson A. Milwood, letters page, *Methodist Recorder*, 2 May 1996, p. 17.
2. Ysenda Maxtone-Graham, cited in 'Raves in naves aim to halt Church exodus', *The Observer*, 7 November 1993, p. 12.
3. The findings of this survey must, however, be treated with caution, since lapsed members were compared with Synod lay representatives, who were much more likely to be office holders than ordinary church members.
4. Gill (1993:9–10), see also Gill (1992:90–117).
5. 'Chattering classes putting faith in the Anglican fold', *The Observer*, 7 April 1996, p. 17.

## 12. Shaping the Future

1. *The Tablet*, 19 August 1995, p. 1050.
2. Joanna Pieters, letters page, *Methodist Recorder*, 13 June 1996.
3. *Leadership*, 18 (1997) pp. 91–3.
4. Useful paperback titles, from a variety of theological perspectives and costing under £10, include: Alister McGrath's *Bridge Building* (Leicester: IVP, 1992), Jim Thompson's *Why God?* (London: Mowbray, 1997) and Peter Vardy's *The Puzzle of God* (London: Fount, 1995) and *The Puzzle of Evil* (London: Fount, 1992).
5. *Wesley's Journal*, 4 March 1738.
6. *The Tablet*, 12 August 1995, p. 1023.
7. 'View from the pew is a vision of health', *The Observer*, 1 December 1996, p. 11.
8. *Greenbelt* (Christian Arts Festival) Internet site @ http://www.green-belt.org.uk/altgrps/altg.html
9. 'Church turns to drink to finance youth services', *The Times*, 15 February 1997.
10. *Alpha News*, February 1997.
11. A *Starter Pack* is available from the Catechumenate Network, Tithings New Barn, Swalcliffe, Banbury, OX15 5DR.
12. *Credo* is available from the Church Union, 7 Tufton Street, London, SW1P 3QN.
13. The *Milestones* study guide is a useful reminder that under-fives also

face important milestones (Muswell Hill: Methodist Division of Education and Youth, 1993).

14. 'In search of the sacred', *Newsweek*, 28 November 1994, pp. 39, 40.
15. 'Tesco's Sunday school special', *The Guardian*, 14 October 1996.
16. Available from *Family Caring Trust*, 44 Rathfriland Road, Newry, County Down, BT34 1LD.
17. 'Family-friendly church?', *Methodist Recorder*, 3 April 1997, p. 14.
18. G. A. Studdert-Kennedy, 'Awake, awake to love and work'.
19. See Dudley and Johnson (1993).
20. See, for instance, the process described by Cole (1990:29–33).
21. 'A different way of doing church' leaflet – part of the Baptist Union *Roots* programme, 1993.

## Appendix: Methodology

1. Our definition is drawn from the study by Hoge, Johnson and Luidens (1993:245).
2. Switchers differ from leavers in some respects – for instance, they are less likely to cite 'loss of faith' as a motive for parting from their previous church – but there is substantial common ground, as previous studies have found (e.g. Hoge 1981:82, 103, 117, 121).

# Bibliography

ABC Television (1964), *Television and Religion*, London, University of London Press.

Abercrombie, N., Baker, J., Brett, S. and Foster, J. (1970), Superstition and religion, the God of the gaps, in D. Martin and M. Hill (eds), *A Sociological Yearbook of Religion in Britain 3*, London, SCM, pp. 93–129.

Ainlay, S.C., Singleton Jr., R. and Swigert, V.L. (1992), Aging and religious participation: reconsidering the effects of health, *Journal for the Scientific Study of Religion*, 31, pp. 175–188.

Albrecht, Stan L., Cornwall, M. and Cunningham, P.H. (1988), Religious leave-taking: disengagement and disaffiliation among Mormons, in David G. Bromley (ed.), *Falling from the Faith: causes and consequences of religious apostasy*, London, Sage, pp. 62–80.

Babinski, Edward T. (1995), *Leaving the Fold: testimonies of former fundamentalists*, New York, Prometheus Books.

Bibby, Reginald W. (1997), Going, going, gone: the impact of geographical mobility on religious involvement, *Review of Religious Research*, 38, pp. 289–307.

Black, Arthur (1928), London church and mission attendances, *The British Weekly*, 1 March.

Brierley, Peter (ed.) (1991), *Prospects for the Nineties: trends and tables from the English church census with denominations and churchmanships*, Eltham, MARC Europe.

Brierley, Peter (1996), *Leaders Briefings No.3: changing churches*, Eltham, Christian Research.

Bromley, David G. (ed.) (1988), *Falling from the Faith: causes and consequences of religious apostasy*, London, Sage.

Bruce, Steve (ed.) (1992), *Religion and Modernization*, Oxford, Clarendon Press.

Bruce, Steve (1995a), *Religion in Modern Britain*, Oxford, Oxford University Press.

Bruce, Steve (1995b), The truth about religion in Britain, *Journal for the Scientific Study of Religion*, 34, pp. 417–430.

Bruce, Steve (1996), *Religion in the Modern World: from cathedrals to cults*, Oxford, Oxford University Press.

Butler, John R. (1966), A sociological study of lapsed membership, *London Quarterly and Holborn Review*, 191, pp. 236–244.

Church of Scotland (1995), Board of Parish Education Report on the decline in numbers of children and young people in the church, to the General Assembly.

Clack, Beverley (1994), Gender and religion, in Philip Richter (ed.), *Social Analysis for Prophets*, Aston, Aston Training Scheme, ch. 8, pp. 1–16.

Cole, John (1990), *How to be a Local Church: an action plan for every Christian*, Bury St Edmunds, Kevin Mayhew.

Coupland, Douglas (1992), *Generation X: tales for an accelerated culture*, London, Abacus Books.

Davey, John (1995), *Burnout: stress in the ministry*, Leominster, Gracewing.

Davie, Grace (1994), *Religion in Britain since 1945: believing without belonging*, Oxford, Blackwell.

Dawkins, Richard (1986), *The Blind Watchmaker*, Harlow, Longman.

Dostoyevsky, Fyodor (1958), *The Brothers Karamazov I*, Harmondsworth, Penguin.

Dudley, Carl S. (1979), *Where Have All Our People Gone? New choices for old churches*, New York, Pilgrim Press.

Dudley, Carl S. and Johnson, Sally A. (1993), *Energising the Congregation: images that shape your church's ministry*, Louisville, Kentucky, Westminster/John Knox Press.

Dulles, Avery (1988), *Models of the Church*, Dublin, Gill and Macmillan.

Fanstone, Michael J. (1993), *The Sheep That Got Away: why do people leave the church?* Tunbridge Wells, MARC.

Finke, Roger and Stark, Rodney (1992), *The Churching of America, 1776–1990: winners and losers in our religious economy*, New Brunswick, Rutgers University Press.

Finnegan, Ruth (1989), *The Hidden Musicians: music-making in an English town*, Cambridge, Cambridge University Press.

Finney, John (1992), *Finding Faith Today: how does it happen?*, Swindon, British and Foreign Bible Society.

Fowler, James W. (1981), *Stages of Faith: the psychology of human development and the quest for meaning*, San Francisco, Harper and Row.

Fowler, James W. (1992), The vocation of faith development theory, in J.W. Fowler, K.E. Nipkow and F. Schweitzer (eds), *Stages of Faith and Religious Development: implications for church, education and society*, London, SCM, pp. 19–36.

Gallup Organisation (1988), *The Unchurched American: 10 years later*, Princeton, Princeton Research Center.

Gaskin, K., Vlaeminke, M. and Fenton, N. (1996), *Young People's Attitudes to the Voluntary Sector*, London, The Commission on the Future of the Voluntary Sector.

General Synod Board of Education (1991), *How Faith Grows: faith development and Christian education*, London, National Society and Church House Publishing.

General Synod Board of Education (1996), *Youth A Part: young people and the church*, London, National Society and Church House Publishing.

General Synod Board of Mission (1996), *The Search for Faith and the Witness of the Church*, London, Church House Publishing.

Giddens, Anthony (1991), *Modernity and Self-Identity: self and society in the late modern age*, Cambridge, Polity Press.

Gill, Robin (1992), Secularization and census data, in S. Bruce (ed.), *Religion and Modernization*, Oxford, Clarendon Press, pp. 90–117.

Gill, Robin (1993), *The Myth of the Empty Church*, London, SPCK.

Grant, John (ed.) (1996), *Sensorama: the new youth culture of intense experience*, London, St Lukes Advertising Agency.

Greeley, Andrew (1992), Religion in Britain, Ireland and the USA, in R. Jowell, L. Brook, G. Prior and B. Taylor (eds), *British Social Attitudes: the 9th report*, Aldershot, Dartmouth, pp. 51–70.

Hadaway, C.K. (1990), *What Can We Do About Church Dropouts?*, Nashville, Abingdon Press.

Hadaway, C.K., Marler, P.L. and Chaves, M. (1993), What the polls don't show: a closer look at US church attendance, *American Sociological Review*, 58, pp. 741–752.

Hadaway, C.K. and Roof, W.C. (1979), Those who stay religious 'nones' and those who don't: a research note, *Journal for the Scientific Study of Religion*, 18, pp. 194–200.

Hale, Russell (1977), *Who are the Unchurched: an exploratory study*, Washington, DC, Glenmary Research Center.

Hampson, Daphne (1990), *Theology and Feminism*, Oxford, Blackwell.

Hartman, Warren J. (1976), *Membership Trends*, Nashville, Discipleship Resources.

Hoge, Dean R. (1981), *Converts Dropouts Returnees: a study of religious change among Catholics*, New York, Pilgrim Press.

Hoge, D.R., Johnson, B. and Luidens, D.A. (1993), Determinants of church involvement of young adults who grew up in Presbyterian churches, *Journal for the Scientific Study of Religion*, 32, pp. 242–255.

Holmes, T.A. and Rahe, R.H. (1967), The social readjustment rating scale, *Journal of Psychometric Research*, 11, pp. 213–218.

Hornsby-Smith, Michael P. (1992), Believing without belonging?, in Bryan Wilson (ed.), *Religion: contemporary issues*, London, Bellew, pp. 125–134.

Howard, Roland (1996), *The Rise and Fall of the Nine O'Clock Service: a cult within the church?*, London, Mowbray.

Hughes, Gerard W. (1985), *God of Surprises*, London, Darton, Longman and Todd.

Hunsberger, Bruce E. (1983), Apostasy: a social learning perspective, *Review of Religious Research*, 25, pp. 21–38.

Hunter III, George G. (1996), *Church for the Unchurched*, Nashville, Abingdon Press.

Hutton, Will (1996), *The State We're In*, London, Vintage.

Iannaccone, Laurence (1992), Religious markets and the economics of religion, *Social Compass*, 39, pp. 123–131.

Iannaccone, Laurence (1994), Why strict churches are strong, *American Journal of Sociology*, 99, pp. 1180–1211.

Jones, Rebecca (1995), *The Difference It Makes: women's stories about how leaving Christianity has affected them*, Lancaster University, unpublished MA thesis.

Kanter, Rosabeth M. (1972), *Commitment and Community*, Cambridge, Massachusetts, Harvard University Press.

Kay, William K. and Francis, Leslie J. (1996), *Drift from the Churches: attitude toward Christianity during childhood and adolescence*, Cardiff, University of Wales Press.

Keillor, Garrison (1994), *The Book of Guys*, London, Faber and Faber.

Kelley, Dean M. (1972), *Why Conservative Churches Are Growing*, New York, Harper and Row.

Kelley, Dean M. (1978), Why conservative churches are still growing, *Journal for the Scientific Study of Religion*, 17, pp. 165–172.

Küng, Hans (1977), *On Being a Christian*, London, Collins.

Levin, Jeffrey S. (1994), Religion and health: is there an association, is it valid, and is it causal? *Social Science and Medicine*, 38, pp. 1475–1482.

Levitt, Mairi A.S. (1996), *Nice When They are Young: contemporary Christianity in families and schools*, Aldershot, Avebury.

McGrath, Alister E. (1992), *Bridge-building: effective Christian apologetics*, Leicester, IVP.

McLuhan, Marshall (1967), *The Medium is the Message*, Harmondsworth, Penguin.

Mathison, John Ed. (1988), *Every Member in Ministry*, Nashville, Discipleship Resources.

Nelsen, Hart M. (1981), Religious conformity in an age of disbelief: contextual effects of time, denomination, and family processes upon church decline and apostasy, *American Sociological Review*, 46, pp. 632–640.

Nipkow, Karl E. (1988), The issue of God in adolescence under growing post-Christian conditions: a Württembergian survey, *Journal of Empirical Theology*, 1, pp. 43–53.

Parks, Sharon D. (1992), The North American critique of James Fowler's theory of faith development, in J.W. Fowler, K.E. Nipkow and F.

Schweitzer (eds), *Stages of Faith and Religious Development: implications for church, education and society,* London, SCM, pp. 101–115.

Parsons, Rob (1995), *The Sixty Minute Father,* London, Hodder and Stoughton.

Peck, M. Scott (1990), *The Different Drum,* London, Arrow Books.

Poore, James C. (1992), *All Change: an exploration of transition,* Peterborough, Methodist Publishing House.

Poxon, Stephen J. (1995), *A Critical Study of Models of University Chaplaincy,* unpublished MTh thesis, Westminster College Oxford.

Ritchie, Karen (1995), *Marketing to Generation X,* New York, Lexington.

Robinson, John (1963), *Honest to God,* London, SCM.

Roof, Wade Clark (1978), *Community and Commitment,* New York, Elsevier.

Roof, Wade Clark (1993), *A Generation of Seekers: the spiritual journeys of the baby boom generation,* San Francisco, HarperSanFrancisco.

Roof, Wade Clark, Carroll, Jackson W. and Roozen, David A. (1995), *The Post-War Generation and Establishment Religion,* Oxford, Westview.

Roof, Wade Clark and Gesch, Lyn (1995), Boomers and the culture of choice: changing patterns of work, family and religion, in N.T. Ammerman and W.C. Roof (eds), *Work, Family, and Religion in Contemporary Society,* New York, Routledge, pp. 61–79.

Roozen, David A. (1980), Church dropouts: changing patterns of disengagement and re-entry, *Review of Religious Research,* 21, pp. 427–450.

Roozen, D.A., McKinney, W. and Thompson W. (1990), The 'big chill' generation warms to worship: a research note, *Review of Religious Research,* 31, pp. 314–323.

Sandomirsky, S. and Wilson, J. (1990), Processes of disaffiliation: religious mobility among men and women, *Social Forces,* 68, pp. 1211–1229.

Savage, John S. (1976), *The Apathetic and Bored Church Member: psychological and theological implications,* New York, LEAD Consultants.

Seyd, P., Whiteley, P. and Parry, J. (1996), *Labour and Conservative Party Members 1990–92: social characteristics, political attitudes and activities,* Aldershot, Dartmouth.

Sherkat, D.E. and Wilson, J. (1995), Preferences, constraints, and choices in religious markets: an examination of religious switching and apostasy, *Social Forces,* 73, pp. 993–1026.

Skonovd, L.N.J. (1979), Becoming apostate: a model of religious defection, paper at Pacific Sociological Association annual meeting, Anaheim, California.

Thomas, Andrew and Finch, Helen (1990), *On Volunteering: a qualitative study of images, motivations and experiences,* London, Volunteer Centre UK.

Thompson, Jim (1997), *Why God?,* London, Mowbray.

Tomlinson, Dave (1995), *The Post-Evangelical,* London, Triangle.

Troeltsch, Ernest (1931), *The Social Teachings of the Christian Churches,* London, George Allen and Unwin.

Vardy, Peter (1992), *The Puzzle of Evil*, London, Fount.

Vardy, Peter (1995), *The Puzzle of God*, London, Fount.

Ward, Hannah and Wild, Jennifer (1995), *Guard the Chaos: Finding Meaning in Change*, London, Darton, Longman and Todd.

Webster, Alison R. (1995), *Found Wanting: women, Christianity and sexuality*, London, Cassell.

Westerhoff, John H. (1976), *Will our Children have Faith?*, New York, Seabury Press.

Wilkinson, H. and Mulgan, G. (1995), *Freedom's Children: work, relationships and politics for 18–34 year olds in Britain today*, London, Demos.

Wilson, J. and Sherkat, D.E. (1994), Returning to the fold, *Journal for the Scientific Study of Religion*, 33, pp. 148–161.

Wink, Walter (1992), *Engaging the Powers: discernment and resistance in a world of domination*, Minneapolis, Fortress Press.

Wright, Frank (1982), *Pastoral Care for Lay People*, London, SCM.

Wright, Stuart A. (1987), *Leaving Cults: the dynamics of defection*, Washington, DC, Society for the Scientific Study of Religion.

Wright, Stuart A. (1988), Leaving New Religious Movements: Issues, theory, and research, in David G. Bromley (ed.), *Falling from the Faith: causes and consequences of religious apostasy*, London, Sage, pp. 143–165.

Wright, Timothy (1994), *A Community of Joy: how to create contemporary worship*, Nashville, Abingdon.

Wuthnow, R. and Christiano, K. (1979), The effects of residential migration on church attendance in the United States, in R. Wuthnow (ed.), *The Religious Dimension: new directions in quantitative research*, New York, Academic Press, pp. 257–276.

# Index of Names

# Index of Subjects